Terrorism and Modern Drama

Terrorism and Modern Drama

edited by
JOHN ORR
and
DRAGAN KLAIĆ

EDINBURGH UNIVERSITY PRESS

© Edinburgh University Press 1990
22 George Square, Edinburgh

Set in Linotron Palatino
by Speedspools, Edinburgh, and
printed in Great Britain by
Page Bros, Norwich

British Library Cataloguing
   in Publication Data
Terrorism and modern drama.
1. Drama in European languages. Special subjects.
Terrorism. Critical studies.
I. Orr, John, 1943–   II. Klaić, Dragan
809.29358

ISBN 0 7486 0173 2
       0 7486 0195 3 pbk

Contents

Acknowledgements

This collection originated in a course held at the Inter-University Centre for Postgraduate Studies in Dubrovnik in September 1988 on 'Politics and Terrorism in Modern Drama'. We would like to thank all the participants there, but particulary Vojin Dimitrijevic, Goran Stefanovski, Dušan Jovanović, Anthony Kubiak and Zoltan Szillassy for their many stimulating comments. We would also like to thank Kathy Wilkes and the Open Society Fund for making several grants available to participating students; Berta Dragicevic and the staff of IUC for their organisational support in Dubrovnik; and the British Council and the University of Arts, Belgrade for their financial help in enabling us as conference organisers and editors to collaborate on this project.

Contributors

DANIEL C. GEROULD is Professor of Theatre Studies and Comparative Literature, City University, New York. He has written and published extensively on dramatic literature, especially French and Polish. He has recently written and edited a volume on American Melodrama, and translated and edited several volumes of plays, essays and documents on the modern theatre.

JOHN ORR is Reader in Sociology at the University of Edinburgh, where he teaches Sociology, Film and Drama. He is the author of *Tragic Realism and Modern Society, Tragic Drama and Modern Society* and *The Making of the Twentieth Century Novel*. He is currently writing a book on tragicomedy and is a theatre critic for *The Literary Review*.

AIDA HOZIC has done her Master's degree at The John Hopkins University, Bologna, on terrorism in Western Europe, and is currently at the University of Virginia.

MICHAEL PATTERSON is Lecturer in Drama at the University of Ulster, Coleraine. He has written mainly on German theatre and his works include *German Theatre Today, The Revolution in German Theatre 1918–33* and *Peter Stein*. He has performed and directed in many countries, including the Malayalam premiere of Brecht's *Caucasian Chalk Circle* in Southern India.

LADO KRALJ is Assistant Professor in Comparative Literature at the University of Ljubljana. He has worked with Richard Schechner's Performance Group and formed the Pekarna theatre group in Ljubljana in 1972. He has also been Artistic Director of the Slovenian National Theatre. His publications include a book on German Expressionism and its impact on Europe, many studies on modernist letters, theatre and art, and translations.

MARY KAREN DAHL is Assistant Professor at the University of Wisconsin at Madison. She was the founder and the director of a programme in computing and civil liberties for Computer Professionals for Social Responsibility, Inc, in Palo Alto. Her book

vii

Political Violence in Drama (UMI Press) was selected as Choice's outstanding academic book of 1987.

DRAGAN KLAIĆ is Professor in the History of Theatre and Dramatic Literature at the University of Belgrade. He was educated at Belgrade and Yale, and has held visiting professorships at the Universities of New Mexico and Pennsylvania. He has published works on F. X. Kroetz, alternative theatre in Yugoslavia, theatre history and dystopian drama. He also worked as a drama critic.

RICHARD BOON is Lecturer in Theatre Studies at the University of Leeds. Following several articles on Howard Brenton, he is currently preparing a full-length study 'Brenton the playwright' (Methuen).

DAVID IAN RABEY is Lecturer in Drama at the University College of Wales, Aberystwyth. He is author of *British and Irish Political Drama in the Twentieth Century* and of the first full-length study of Howard Barker (Macmillan).

SUSANNE GREENHALGH is Lecturer in Drama at the Roehampton Institute, London.

Terrorism and Drama: Introduction

Terrorism is almost impossible to define. In general terms, it is violent action intended for public effect which is usually directed against members or institutions of the state. But it may also be directed against random sections of the population. Often, its intention is to hurt not only its key victims but also those who support them. When its targets are those in power, the intention is to threaten the whole power structure. When the targets are the followers of the powerful, often the attempt is to threaten other like-minded followers. In whatever guise, terrorism exists to encourage assumed sympathisers and discourage the enemy. It is used to create a climate of fear in which people are powerless to act, and to give the terrorist a covert power. But often it works only in the short run. Terrorists can be isolated or betrayed or they can be ignored by those whose support they wish to gain. They can fall victim in turn to state terror which summons up much more in the way of resources, and develops its own methods of surveillance, punishment and reprisal. Terrorist outrages may be directed against selected enemies within the state apparatus, or against those who are only 'guilty by association', who have cooperated with those the terrorists define as their enemies. For most terrorists, all innocence is relative, and the definition of 'collaboration' is elastic. For those passers-by killed or maimed in terrorist bombings, for example, the ultimate rationalisation is reserved: they failed to take the necessary precautions. They were in the wrong place at the wrong time.

Definition is difficult and there can be no value-free discussion of terrorism.[1] One country's freedom-fighter can be another's terrorist. But there is one interesting area of agreement. Many commentators have noted the almost theatrical nature of terrorism in the contemporary world. Its varied use of bombings, hijackings, kidnappings and assassinations involves the planned staging of events which turn unwary publics into involuntary audiences, into the hostages, so to speak, of bloody spectacle. Such actions are nearly always defended in terms of ultimate political goals, of the overthrow of a particular state or a particular government or a specific government policy. At the same time, their immediate aim is to foment outrages which 'audiences' everywhere cannot ignore and to which the direct enemies of the terrorist, those in high office of the beseiged state, must respond. It is no coincidence that terrorism has been perceived over the last twenty years as a world-wide phenomenon, as an integral part of an audio-visual electronic age in which all information is potentially global, and can be instantly transmitted and shown simultaneously in different countries throughout the world. The theatre, in turn, has taken due note of such theatricality and made terrorist spectacle a major theme in contemporary drama. This, then, is the starting-point of this volume. Acts of violence against property or people are staged for different audiences simultaneously, sometimes to frighten, often to intimidate, usually to provoke the state enemy into excessive and unpopular counter-terror, but always to ensure that the act itself cannot be ignored. Such outrages would be nothing without their dramatic impact. They are the unlikely fusion of two contradictory things: spectacle and secrecy. Terrorists need their actions to have, literally and metaphorically, an explosive impact, but they themselves must remain inaccessible and their methods unpredictable. No one must know where they will strike next. They lurk in the wings, hoping their timing and precision will land them in centre stage.

To pursue the metaphor further, terrorism uses a moveable stage and its actors are often invisible. Its state enemies can reply either by suppressing the event as a public happening and replying with counter-terror or, where faced with a more open flow of public information, by giving an official version of events and actually turning its high-risk theatricality into a controlled political spectacle. In this way, state and media authorities endeavour to stage-manage the terrorist spectacle and make the terrorist act a source of widespread moral outrage, flooding the press and electronic media with melo-dramas of suffering and denunciation which are intended to turn the weapon of publicity against its perpetrators, and staging elaborate trials of arrested suspects to present them as monsters beyond the pale. It seems natural, therefore, that drama should concern itself with a terrorism that is theatrical and with counter-responses which range from counter-terror to the stage-management of political spectacles. Terrorism here is two things, both *event*, the things that happen, and *process*, that is to say, it consists of the relationships develop-ing among protagonists, the dyadic relationship of terrorists and authorities, and the triadic relationship of state, terrorists and public. Finally, all this is selectively perceived in different ways in the world beyond the state's boundaries. At all these levels, the desire of terrorists to create violent outrage and promote fear makes them a subject for the theatre. As a public event, terrorism is paratheatrical, a performance with an involuntary audience, a happening with an unscripted sce-nario that can go badly wrong, and often does. The dramatic text introjects aspects of this performative element back into a formal arena of performance, the modern stage.

This process must be set into a historical context. Terrorism as the systematically secret production of a theatre of cruelty may be a permanent feature of our own age, but political terror *per se* has a long history in the development of the modern state. Without the complexities of modern state terror, terrorism itself would never have evolved. In Western drama, such terror in its early forms has been a powerful constituent of Renaissance tragedy and has moved forward into new and varied dramatic forms right down into the twentieth century. The development of abstract political ideologies since 1789 has here been crucial. Several contributors to the present volume have traced that lineage and the fascination that it has held for modern society.

Daniel Gerould puts this development into historical per-spective by illustrating the fascination of the Elizabethans with terror as a weapon of state power. Gerould's discussion is a salutary reminder not only that terror has always been a

weapon of the powerful, but also that the growing centralisation of the modern state has given it added potential. The
fascination that Tamburlaine held for Christopher Marlowe,
the government spy, or that Richard III held for Shakespeare
remind us that Renaissance tragedy has its origins in Tudor
terror and in the embryonic British state as much as in the
Italian city-state of Machiavelli. But, as Gerould points out,
the systematic ideological use of terror is ushered in, centuries
later, with the French Revolution. This is the intellectual origin
of the systematic terror we today call terrorism, the organised
use of terror reputedly in the service of a holistic creed.
Gerould shows the fascination of the figure of Robespierre as
the first ideologue of terror in the plays of Georg Büchner in
the nineteenth century and of Stanisława Przybyszewska in
the twentieth, the Polish playwright viewing her French revolutionary hero very much from the perspective of a different
kind of revolution in 1917. If terror has been with us throughout European civilisation, then terrorism, its modern offshoot,
has been with us just as constantly throughout the twentieth
century and has now become global. It is the offshoot of an
age of ideology in which terror is seen, often wrongly, as an
instrument by which revolutionary struggle may be acceler-
ated. When it is seen as *the* instrument to further that struggle,
all the signs point to an ignominious collapse of revolutionary
ideals.

It must be remembered that the dividing line between terror and terrorism is sometimes very fine. Marx's contempt for
Nechayev and his group's nihilistic use of terrorism in Russia
was part of his assault on the anarchist strategies of Bakunin
which he felt had no power to mobilise the working classes.
While rejecting, in the same spirit, the terrorist outrages of
secret conspiratorial groups, Leninists were later to assume
that terror is often a necessary resort of mass class-struggle
during revolution or civil war. Despite their strong rejection
of indiscriminate outrages, such as the spectacular bombings and assassinations of the Russian Social-Revolutionaries.
the Bolsheviks regarded rational terror, the use or threat of
violence to intimidate people away from support of counter-
revolutionaries, as a legitimate weapon of class struggle in a
revolutionary situation. Similarly, localised terror was used

by the Vietcong in the Vietnamese war of liberation although it was in no way comparable to the systematic mass terror of the Khmer Rouge once they seized power in Kampuchea. By contrast, most recent terrorism in the West, limited by its failure to gain mass support, has often become an end in itself. Its limited theatre of war pushes its political goals further and further into the distance as they repel potential sympathisers.

Terrorism, therefore, cannot always be wished away purely as the last resort of those who have failed to mobilise mass support, as some liberal critics have attempted.[2] On the other hand, it cannot be written off as the practice of desperadoes who have no beliefs at all, as some conservative critics have supposed.[3] But in the Europe and North America of the last twenty-five years, most forms of terror have had little direct connection with mass uprising. They *have* been the resort of those who have effectively abandoned the political struggle for mass support. Contemporary terrorism is dystopian, arising from the active and at times cynical despair of those who still believe. The terrorism of groups who call themselves revolutionary is often not revolutionary at all, since these groups lack popular support and, after continued failure to attain it, finally lose the will to try and generate it altogether. Moreover, the terrorists' failure to persuade is often compounded by violence meaningless to those it is meant to attract. Most terrorists, in effect, put the cart before the horse. Terrorist despair need not be conscious, and usually is not, but in terrorism's fanatical militancy, there is a strongly schizoid and self-destructive element. Moreover, the self-image of the terrorist as a lonely martyr for the common cause or as a self-appointed agent of radical change makes him act as a spasmodic performer on the larger stage of society. At the same time, it makes him an engrossing model for the maverick yet threatening protagonist of modern drama, an up-to-date variant of the villain or malcontent of Renaissance drama, or of the marginal hero of romantic tragedy.

The revolutionary dilemma of having to choose between terrorism and mass uprising, or of trying to *avoid* having to choose between them, has been a vital theme in German political theatre. The historical origins of the theme

of terrorism is explored by Michael Patterson in his essay
on Piscator's staging of Schiller's *Die Rauber* and on the dis-
section of revolutionary terror by Brecht in *Die Massnahme*.
Patterson suggests that Schiller's piece of 1780 can be seen
as one of the first 'terrorist' plays in the European reper-
toire, a claim reinforced by Piscator's use of modern dress
in his 1926 production. The key test of Piscator's imaginative
transfer comes, according to Patterson, in the portrayal of
Spiegelberg, the villain of the anarchist band, who is used
by the director to test the true goals of Karl Moor, the leader, and who effectively turns the robbers into a terrorist
group. In Brecht's controversial political drama, which many
critics have seen as a pro-Stalinist tract, the murder of the
Young Comrade by his fellow-Communists – with his full
acquiescence – raises the whole question of the rationality of
terror, and the play explores the shifting boundary between
terror and terrorism within the Communist Party of the thirties.

In looking at a different dimension of the German theatre,
pre- and post-war Expressionism, Lado Kralj shows how its
apocalyptic strain, its desperate wish (which has strong Christian and Romantic overtones) for a new dawning in modern
society, inadvertently yields up a new terrorist sensibility.
The cosmic transfer of apocalypse into nihilism which takes
place through the powerful influence of Nietzsche (and above
all, through his prophetic dismembering of bourgeois society)
works here through a 'revolution of the mind' which desires
to be real in its consequences. One of the quintessential
forms of individual anarchistic revolt in Expressionism is
parricide as a political act, a stark, uncompromising theme in
key plays by Reinhard Sorge. Walter Hasenclaver and Arnolt
Bronnen. The subsequent theme of collective revolt, written
in close proximity to the experience of the 1918 revolution,
is the province of Ernst Toller and Georg Kaiser. Here Kralj
sees a movement towards collectivist utopia which is already
undermined by the role of the charismatic leader in plays such
as *Masse-Mensch* and *Gas*, where the latter eventually terrorises
and destroys those he seeks to embody in his role as the maker
of a new world.

It is in the period some time after the Second World War,

however, that terrorism became a more systematic and widespread phenomenon among groups failing to attain political power. In effect, it is with the fury of the Algerian War, the escalation of the Vietnamese War and the Arab–Israeli conflict in the Middle East that it started to become salient. The first major terrorist group on European soil in this period was the OAS (Organisation de l'Armée secrète), which carried its secret counter-revolutionary war against the Algerian FLN (Front de Libération nationale) onto the French mainland, and tried to assassinate de Gaulle and destabilise the Fifth Republic. But the other major historical phenomena in France so crucial to the development of terrorism were the 'Events of May' in Paris in 1968, the utopian enthusiasm of which spread in one form or another throughout Europe during the rest of that fateful year.

Aida Hozic and Dragan Klaić both look at different consequences of that complex and influential period, one from the standpoint of politics, the other from the standpoint of contemporary Yugoslav drama. Hozic makes several vital points about contemporary terrorism which cannot be overstressed. Terrorism, she points out, is a developing phenomenon which undergoes its own historical changes. At first, when it fails to gain the publicity it seeks, it escalates its actions from the ritual humiliation or kidnapping of victims to bombings and murders. Its power to create a theatrical impact depends on the reception of its actions and, in particular, on the importance accorded to those actions by the authorities. It is they who decide whether or not to turn the paratheatrical nature of terror into ordained spectacle, to enlarge its 'audience' beyond those who witness its violent outrages first-hand. In this way, authorities turn the paratheatricality back on its perpetrators. They try to demonstrate that it is 'bad' theatre. In her important and engrossing essay, Hozic traces the escalation of terrorism in Western Europe in the early seventies in terms of its increasing violence and in terms of the propagandistic counter-reponse of the state and the national media. She concludes, however, that the meaning of terrorism is never straightforward. It is a complex phenomenon whose actions hold different messages for different groups of people.

Klaić focuses more closely on the ideological development

of terrorism. He sees the subsequent two decades after 'Sixty-Eight' as a dystopian period in European culture. After the initial euphoria of Sixty-Eight began gradually to evaporate throughout Europe, the emergent terrorists, the new utopians, appeared as *ultimate* utopians, the 'last believers in dreams no-one wants to take seriously any longer'. One of the most important dramatic commentators on this diffusion of revolt into self-defeating rage has been the Yugoslav playwright Dušan Jovanović. Klaić analyses the different elements of ludism and self-conscious theatricality in Jovanović's work which has forged a new dramatic form out of the unlikely marriage of utopianism and terror. In *Play out of a Tumour in the Brain, or Polluting the Air* (1971–72) the playwright shows a palace revolution within a conventional theatre, which then turns into an avant-garde commune, as an example of deranged utopia producing a mini-concentration camp barricaded against hostile authorities in the world outside. In his later plays, Jovanović deals equally with the ideological apparatus of the state which undermines utopian aspirations and with the irrational impulses of its followers which subvert the utopian desire for reason.

If terrorism can be seen as paratheatrical, as a form of social drama, the question of its dramatic form in the theatre becomes vital. How does one turn something latently theatrical into actual theatre? John Orr argues that one of the attractions of terrorism to playwrights is its dramatic impact, which can be both immediate and sensational in its repercussions. In particular, the violent attack on the state presents a direct challenge for political dramatists. However, the most effective playwrights are those who manage to blend the immediacy of the event with the distancing effected by theatrical techniques. These differ greatly from the techniques of documentary and media reportage. Dario Fo's use of farce, and Genet, Hampton and Soyinka's use of tragicomedy, point up the absurdities of the terrorist situation and also the human faillibility of those involved in its masquerades. The historical dramas of Bond and Brenton use temporal distance to generate political perspective. They demand critical judgement through their use of Brechtian alienation techniques, but also involvement through their use of 'Aggro-effects'. Dramas of contemporary terrorism which adhere more closely to naturalistic conventions often remain too close to their subject and become, emotionally speaking, too melodramatic.

The essays by Richard Boon and David Rabey both emphasise the central role which terrorism has played in the revitalisation of the British theatre in the seventies. Boon looks closely at the work of Howard Brenton, one of the key English playwrights of that decade, and locates the origins of his work in the Situationist spectacles of 1968. The hero-terrorist of Brenton's early plays shows the influence of Situationism, but in *Magnificence* Brenton rejects the terrorist at the same time as his work moves from oppositional theatre practice to more mainstream work. In *Magnificence*, unlike in his later plays, Brenton's hero dominates the action and though his author rejects him politically he allows him to command the stage theatrically. In Brenton's early work, history is disregarded or judged to be hostile to the 'society of spectacle'. The later plays, however, insist on the need to confront history and learn from the past.

Rabey deals more generally with images of terrorism in British drama of the seventies and the eighties. His essay broadens the scope of the dilemma originating in Brenton's *Magnificence*, that of the degree to which the hero-terrorist is integrated within a wider network of terrorists or ultimately isolated from it. Rabey looks, therefore, at the problems of isolation and commitment in the terrorist cell and goes on to examine Bond's *The Worlds*, Griffiths' *Real Dreams*, Hutchinson's *Rat in the Skull* and Howard Barker's *Credentials of a Sympathiser* and *That Good Between Us*. The collectivist view of a politically subversive network, Rabey argues, must invariably conflict with the traditional elevation of the solitary dramatic hero and the division of the public and the private which is implied by the heroic tradition.

Mary Karen Dahl focuses less on the dramatic profile of the terrorist and more on the dramatic response to state terror in the contemporary world. Looking specifically at Fo's *Accidental Death of an Anarchist*, Athol Fugard's *Statements After an Arrest Under the Immorality Act* and Ronald Harwood's *The Deliberate Death of a Polish Priest*, she sees world theatre in different ways as a focus of resistance to state terror since, as an art form, it is both a public and a communal event. Spectators in the theatre audience can feel part of a collective community of resistance to terror whether or not they are the direct recipients, and whether or not they live within the particular country whose terror the play defines. Dahl opposes the spontaneous community of the oppositional theatre to the fabricated 'value community' which the state tries to create through intimidation and fear. In a state governed by terror, the theatre is one of the few repositories of authentic communal value, an authentic form of human defiance.

One of the features of contemporary terrorism in the West has been the significantly high number of woman involved in small terrorist groups, both in the planning and in the execution of terrorist outrages. This has in turn produced a response from female playwrights such as Anne Devlin, Caryl Churchill and Franca Rame. In her powerful and challenging discussion of the female terrorist in contemporary drama, Suzanne Greenhalgh raises gender as a central issue. She looks at the way political terror is gendered by means of language, imagery, action and the deployment of male and female roles. She rejects the notion that women caught up in terrorism are portrayed as 'token terrorists' or as mere symbols or ciphers. Terrorism, she argues, offers a challenging field for a much more complex portrayal of changing gender roles in Western societies, and give credence to recent feminist theories of a 'maternal theatre'.

In conclusion, we can argue that terrorism has vital connections to drama for two reasons. The first, as we have reiterated, is the violent and often macabre nature of its theatricality which cannot fail to attract our best dramatists. The second is that, like modernity itself, it has become 'our fate'. It is an alternative and lesser fate than that of rationalisation about which Max Weber, Theodor Adorno, Jürgen Habermas and others have spoken and which is central to our understanding of the advanced industrial world. It is in fact a defiance of rationalisation, a form of disenchantment radically different from that complex phenomenon Weber had simplistically called 'charisma'. It is about disorder and not order, irrationality and not reason, the unpredictable rather than the obvious, the horrifying rather than the mundane, all of which are aspects of the experience that modern playwrights since the Symbolists has attempted to capture and portray. Terror has no great leaders no real figureheads, although it has its own mythology, or rather, the topoi, the character types, the obligatory scenes the patterns of resolution that come to constitute a dramaturgy of political violence. All subsequently enter the dramaturgy of the contemporary political theatre. Some members of its networks may attain notoriety but more often they remain anonymous or are quickly forgotten by name. In a world where international relations are relatively stable but nations themselves are more and more threatened by the grievances of regions and peripheries; in continents where wars between nations have thankfully been abandoned but where nuclear war still threatens, terrorism is an incubus which will survive as the last resort of violent disenchantment, which can function efficiently and wage small-scale technological warfare. It is a pathology which has become a normality. It can be held in check but not eliminated. It is now a sporadic but permanent spectacle in our audio-visual lives, briefly turning the world of information into a world of livid sensation, but in the end achieving little except the short-lived creation of the theatrical event it has briefly become.

NOTES

1. We are grateful in this section to Vojin Dimitrijevic's paper 'The Notion of Terrorism' given at the symposium on 'Politics and Terrorism in Modern Drama' at the Inter-University Centre, Dubrovnik in September 1988. The etymology of 'terror' and 'terrorism' is discussed by Walter Lacqueur in his book *Terrorism* (London: Weidenfeld and Nicholson, 1977), 4ff.
2. The most important liberal critique of terrorism is Richard Rubenstein's *Alchemists of Revolution: Terrorism in the Modern World* (New York: Basic Books, 1988), which includes a very precise discussion of the dilemmas of political activists who resort to terror as a method of revolutionary mobilisation. The *locus classicus* of current academic work on terrorism is Thomas Perry Thornton 'Terror as a Weapon of Political Agitation' in Harry Eckstein, ed., *Internal War* (New York: Free Press, 1963), 71-100, 2.

3. The Conservative critique of terrorism concerns itself mainly with the vulnerabilities of the liberal state and the
   effectiveness of security measures against different forms
   of terrorism. For one of the most lucid examples, see Paul
   Wilkinson, *Terrorism and the Liberal State*, 2nd ed. (London,
   Macmillan, 1986).

PART I

History and Context

1

Terror, the Modern State and the Dramatic Imagination

DANIEL GEROULD

'Terror and civilisation are inseparable' – I take as my point of departure this proposition developed by Max Horkheimer and Theodor Adorno in their *Dialectic of Enlightenment*. 'Culture has developed with the protection of the executioner', the theoreticians of the Frankfurt School admit, with apparent reluctance and regret. 'It is impossible to abolish terror and retain civilisation. Even a lessening of terror implies a beginning of the process of dissolution.'[1]

The interactions of terror and civilisation have served as recurring themes in Western drama. The jarring conjunction of seeming opposites has elicited ambivalent responses in playwrights attracted to the paradox of the executioner and his allies – the policeman, spy informer, secret agent – as the defender of culture. Revelation of the face of terror beneath the mask of civilisation is a theatrical moment of disturbing power, whether the dramatist exults in the violence, apologises for it, or laments it. In order to anatomise major aspects of state terror as depicted in drama, I must move freely back and forth between historical eras and their artistic representation. Dramatisations of civilisation's complicity with terror sometimes follow, sometimes anticipate political events and social realities.

Although terror and civilisation may always be inseparably linked, there have been three periods of highly advanced European culture during which the connection has proved particularly fruitful for drama – if not at the time, then when perceived from a later perspective. These are the age of Tudor despotism, the Reign of Terror during the French Revolution,

15

and the era of war, revolution, and dictatorship in the early twentieth century. In all these instances, terror became a principal means of governing; sometimes it also became the end itself, even though, ostensibly, its purpose was to maintain the status quo or to install a new revolutionary regime.[2]

1. *Tudor Tyranny*

It was in the Renaissance with the rise of the modern European nation-states that repressive terrorism first displayed its full range of techniques. Absolute monarchs and ambitious rivals seeking to displace them were the terrorists; subjects of the state, caught between these unbridled forces, were the terrorised. Violence was indisputably necessary to sustain civilisation; severed heads on pikes were every-day visual evidence of this. The gaining and holding of power depended on terror; the state existed by virtue of its ability to terrorise its enemies, internal and external, real or imagined.

But in the new Tudor nation-state there was an obsessive fear of treason on the part of the power-holders who saw history as a vast conspiracy. Indeed, paranoia was a national hysteria. In Henry VIII's embryonic police state, informers were everywhere, or at least people thought they were, and espionage was part of the social structure.[3] Everyone was suspect; and innocence was no safeguard. It was enough to be accused of thinking treasonable thoughts to go to the block. At the last moment, the condemned typically admitted to heinous crimes, as a final act of self-sacrifice to the power of the state, no matter how false the charges or fabricated the evidence. Once found guilty by the law, the victim was considered by all, even by himself, as worthy to die.[4] Just as their counterparts in the Moscow show trials some four hundred years later, these Elizabethan traitors confessed on the scaffold to their involvement in foreign conspiracies and died proclaiming their devotion to sovereign and country. In both cases, the terrorist mechanism (far more powerful than physical torture) was propelled by the belief in the absolute supremacy of the state over the individual and the doctrine of total obedience to the will of society.[5]

The roots of modern drama dealing with state terror are to be found in the plays of Marlowe and of Shakespeare, who regarded with a mixture of horror, awe and admiration the great terrorist rulers and usurpers. Elizabethan police spy and secret agent, Christopher Marlowe was fascinated by the terrorist mentality embodied in ruthlessly ambitious individuals. His *Tamburlaine* was – and still is – shocking in its unmasking of state power, stripping it of any semblance of legitimacy, legal or divine, and revealing its cruel natural basis – and ultimate futility – in superior might. The Scythian shepherd's rise to power and world domination reveals the 'mechanisms of conquest and repression' that Camus found in Hitler's nihilistic state terrorism: belief in nothing but action, unadulterated dynamism, perpetual motion in the crushing of new enemies.[6] The spectator is placed in an uneasy position vis-à-vis the Scythian strong man, compelled to admire Tamburlaine for his 'instinct of domination' and 'gangster morality'; Tamburlaine is a more efficient and stylish terrorist than any of the lawful monarchs he supplants, who are equally bloodthirsty, yet hypocritical and inept in their barbarity.

It is hardly possible to talk of Tamburlaine's abuse of power, since the tyrant's very ability to rule is measured by the arbitrary and excessive pain he inflicts upon his enemies. Suffering is the other side of power.[7] The Emperor of the Turks, Bajazeth, is kept in a cage and fed scraps from the conqueror's table; periodically, he is brought forth to serve as a footstool as Tamburlaine mounts his throne. Such a calculated public display of inhumanity is designed to teach the world that Tamburlaine can, with impunity, challenge the laws of gods and men. Chivalric respect for one's opponent has been replaced by degradation and humiliation. In *Edward II*, Marlowe pursues to new extremes his fascination with violence and examines the mechanisms of pure terror as though they were ordered by exact, natural laws like those governing the physical universe. In the course of the play, the arbitrary but ineffective terrorist king becomes himself the victim, imprisoned and tortured to death. The location of the scene of ultimate terror is no longer public, but a damp and gloomy dungeon beneath Berkeley Castle, polluted by its sewers, where the executioner, Lightborn, with his prosaic but hideous instruments – table, featherbed, red-hot spit, and ditch water – violates the wretched king exposed in all his naked vulnerability. Here the forecast is of the methods of the twentieth-century secret police; we are reminded of the atrocities suffered by prisoners in the concentration camps of the Second World War.

For Marlowe what was most theatrical could only be found in those moments of psycho-physiological terror overwhelming the isolated individual when one can see right through the veils of civilisation to the very bottom of nature's cruelty. Shakespeare, on the other hand, traces in his first sequence of history plays the origins and consequences of dynastic terrorism among warring factions of nobles as all familial and societal relationships are gradually corrupted. The three *Henry VI* plays – long dismissed as spurious, or patronised as crude apprentice-work, because they do not give priority to the development of character – have been rediscovered, after our experience of mid-twentieth-century atrocities, as incisive political theatre charting the rise of terrorism and its inevitable course.

In the tetralogy made up of the three parts of *Henry VI* together with *Richard III*, the action moves, at first gradually but soon rapidly and savagely, from an ancient chivalric order, whose traditional forms of ceremony are subverted, to a ruthless modern system in which the only legitimation is that of superior terror; all sense of who has the best legal and moral right to the succession is lost in a whirlwind of violence. What terror does to the social fabric is of central concern in *Henry VI*, Part II; husband and wife, apprentice and master, brother and brother, and father and son are set against one another. With the gruesome murder by strangulation of the Lord Chancellor, legal authority crumbles and competing terrorisms are let loose. While the rival warlords practice politic assassination, Jack Cade's roving bands of workmen – butchers, weavers, sawyers – aping their betters, stage their own rebellion and terrorise the citizens of London with random killings.

Jack Cade's uprising is a genuine social revolution, designed to overturn the existing civilisation and replace it with an inverted hierarchy of values. In Cade's new world, everything will be its opposite: 'Let the magistrates be labouring men; / and therefore should we be magistrates.'[8] Cade and his levellers are the first instance in European drama of the mob as an instrument of revolutionary terror, and although their revolt is viewed from a perspective that automatically condemns it as vicious and absurd, Shakespeare presents its violence as a direct consequence and mirror image of the terrorism of the state; in instituting their utopia, the revolutionary mob's actions are a parody, reconstruction, and new creation of the old government's mode of operation.[9]

In their reaction to the repressive civilisation produced by human reason, Cade and his followers decide to kill all lawyers, destroy books and records, and make it a crime to know how to read and write. The workmen have seen the abuses of a corrupt system and, with a frightening consistency, wish to do away with society altogether in order to do away with its inequities. Their attempted destruction of law and order is a consequence of the perversion of justice in the highest places, and their uprising simply follows, in a more chaotic and extreme fashion, the example set by the contentious nobles. In all his dealings, Cade proceeds by a kind of insane logic which reflects and reduces to absurdity the conflicting claims of the ambitious warlords. His terrorist slogan, 'Kill and knock down', is matched by Richard's accurate perception, at the beginning of his rise to the throne, that 'princes kill'.[10] Cade's new principle of government, 'But then are we in order when we are most out of order',[11] describes precisely not only his own straggling anarchic troops, but also the whole course of the dynastic struggles with their endless perjuries, betrayals, and changing of allegiances. All the mob's worst atrocities are paralleled and exceeded by the desecration of corpses, the vengeful killing of children, and the humiliation and torture of prisoners practised by the ruling class. In fact, Cade and the mob adopt the aristocratic mode of ritual killing by decapitation, followed by terrorist displays of heads on poles. After having Lord Treasurer Say and his son-in-law Cromer beheaded, Cade orders his henchmen to manipulate the poles, explaining, 'Let them kiss one another; for they loved well when they were alive'.[12] The severed head held up on a pike, is the emblem of Tudor terrorism, whether practised by the nobles or the people. In the violent and chaotic world of *Henry VI*, in which England plunges into insane brutality, heads begin to appear everywhere on battlements and poles.

Although Richard III, both before and after ascending the throne, sends a number of his friends and enemies to the block, he is above all a master of dissimulation, artfully creating an atmosphere of fear and suspicion by 'tales and whisperings' (to quote Bacon), setting brother against brother and faction against faction. Thus Richard incites King Edward to imprison Clarence for treason and then has his brother secretly murdered in the tower. In his securing of power in act III, Richard – aided by Buckingham, who will later on be eliminated in his turn – uses every totalitarian trick to 'persuade' the Mayor and Citizens of London to accept the usurper as legitimate king. All the modern terrorist techniques of political violence, rabble-rousing and aggressive propaganda are known to the hunchbacked dissembler: smears against rivals trumped-up charges about dangerous associates; the removal of potential opponents; false promises and feigned laments for betrayed friends; accusations against the dead; predated death sentences; staged rallies and organised enthusiasm;[13] provoked crises and fabricated states of alert (Gloucester and Buckingham appear 'in rotten armour, marvellous ill-fitting' and pretend to drive off imaginary attackers); and feigned piety and reluctance to rule (Richard enters with 'two right reverent Fathers', reading the Holy Book).[14] The tyrant-terrorist manipulates reality and appearance through an equivocal and misleading use of language. To allay suspicion, the dictator knows how to feign geniality (as in Richard's good-humoured inquiry about strawberries); to terrify, he can simulate a towering rage (as in his accusations against Hastings). All is fraudulent, for the tyrant is an actor.

Shakespeare's early history plays often provided a model for such modern playwrights as Büchner Witkiewicz (or Witkacy), and Brecht in their portrayal of terrorism. For example, Brecht sent his Arturo Ui to school to study Richard III, whose methods of eliminating opponents become an inspiration for the Chicago gangster. 'Doesn't he make you think of Richard the Third?' Brecht asks in the prologue.

In his later history plays, Shakespeare is less concerned with the terrorism of governing, or at least less open in his unmasking of it. In the patriotic and celebratory *Henry V*, Shakespeare seemingly puts the best possible face on a military imperialist whose claims to his own throne are shaky and whose war of conquest in France is of dubious legality. His crafty elimination of enemies, his coldblooded orders to kill French prisoners of war, and his clever manipulation of his own troops have led some critics to see Henry V as a master dissembler sharing certain traits with Richard III, or even as an insincere, unscrupulous killer masquerading as a national hero.[15] Shakespeare cannot conceive of a statesman or a state that is not terrorist, giving to even his most flattering portraits of rulers a chilling undertone.

2. *Signs and Symbols of Terror*

In *The History of Richard III* – which painted the fifteenth-century monarch from the house of York as a misshapen terrorist in order to justify Tudor claims to the throne – Sir Thomas More characterises politics as a king's game 'for the most part played upon scaffolds',[16] on which stage the humanist scholar and statesman will later meet his own doom, another victim of Henry VIII's despotism. Beheading on the scaffold was Elizabethan terror theatricalised. A stage is raised in public view, an audience assembled as witnesses and spectators. The condemned plays the principal role; other actors include the executioner and his assistants, priest, and presiding court officials who read the charges. The performance occurs at a fixed time and place, and the blow will fall on a specified part of the body, where head may be neatly severed from neck. Meeting death in such circumstances offers opportunities for a display of histrionics during which memorable final words are spoken. For the privileged players in the game of politics, state terror had its rituals and ceremonial forms, allowing of a heightened rhetoric and self-dramatisation at the moment of death. In Shakespearean drama the block and axe were unseen, but ever present.

In 1789 a radical change took place in the ritual of terror. Although it did not immediately produce any drama of significance – Jean Starobinski points out that 'revolutions do not immediately discover an artistic language corresponding to the new political order'[17] – the French Revolution systematised and modernised terror; in fact, it gave the term its modern significance and shaped all future understanding of the concept. The fall of the Bastille led to the rise of the modern terrorist state with its centralised power, mass conscripted army, economic, political, and social controls, organised secret police, informers, and spies, and scientific and technological bases. Although the old executioner, Charles Henri Sanson and Son, was retained, an amazing new instrument was introduced that captured the popular imagination. Terror, now administered democratically, by the people, found its perfect expression in the hypnotic public spectacle offered by this new killing machine, the guillotine.

The use of terror in 1793–94 differed from that of the *ancien régime* in that it was no longer aimed at maintaining the privileged position of a few individuals; it was terror in the name of all. Democratic terror gave voice to the sovereign will of the people, from which no dissent or appeal was possible. It was as infallible as the blade that fell swiftly and suddenly; the action of the guillotine was as single, unified, and total as the people's will. It was terror by committee, by acclamation, by popular demand. A model invention of the Enlightenment, the guillotine was designed to make capital punishment quick, painless, and humane. Efficient and semi-automatic, the new gadget promoted mass production. 'Facility begat use, and multitudes were sent to the other world merely because it had become so very easy to send them.'[18] Once the technological means were available to speed up the killing, more and more people had to be killed. The ritualising of terror gave way to its mechanisation.

Terror took to the streets, spread riotously throughout the city, became entertainment. Seats could be booked, dancing took place around the guillotine as around a Maypole, and toy models were sold for children. Madame Tussaud made death masks from the freshly decapitated heads of both Louis XVI and Robespierre; crowds flocked to see the wax models in her *Cabinet de Cire*. The machine took precedence over the executioner, depersonalising killing and rendering it technically neutral. Sanson, the Parisian executioner, remained a figure respected by royalists and revolutionaries alike. The executioner was now simply a technician running a machine.

In fact, during the reign of terror a member of the Convention proposed a new statute whereby the professional stigma would be removed from actors and executioners.[19]

During the French Revolution, terror not only went into the streets but also became a public enterprise, to which every citizen was urged to contribute. As an expression of the people's unified will, the Reign of Terror demanded the participation of all. Hence the compulsive publicity characteristic of the time. 'Public vigilance and denunciation were institutionalized in the Terror.'[20] Informing was a virtuous act, a civic duty. The festival of blood around the guillotine permitted the release of centuries-old hatreds and resentments and an open-air enactment of fantasies of vengeance long repressed. Terrorism was a spectacular orgy, by means of which virtue was extolled and vice castigated. After the fall of Robespierre in 1794, reaction to extreme revolutionary ideology set in. The guillotine went into semi-retirement while at the same time its iconography entered popular culture at all levels. Under the Directory, among the gilded youth that flourished as a result of war profiteering, *bals des victimes* were fashionable, at which the chic hair-style was *à la victime* as though sheared for the blade, with a thin band of red silk worn around the neck.[21]

By the time of Louis Philippe, the guillotine, which once had given long-running performances in the great squares of Paris, had been put away, to be taken out furtively only on the morning of an execution in front of the prison where the condemned awaited his punishment. Croker writes, 'The Executions . . . took place at early hours and in remote and uncertain places; and every humane art was used to cover the operations of the fatal instrument with a modest veil, not only from motives of general decency and humanity, but also, no doubt, from national pride and . . . sensibility'.[22] In other words, terror that had proclaimed itself proudly and publicly during the Revolution, now partially hid itself and was exercised more discretely. Terrorism passed into the hands of the police and worked behind closed doors.

In later periods of repression renewed interest has always been kindled in the events of 1789; all nineteenth-century revolutionary spirits find both inspiration and cautionary lessons in the continuity of their struggles with those of Marat,

Danton, and Robespierre. The French Revolution becomes the
measure of all future deliberations on terror and civilisation.

Representations of the workings of the guillotine on stage –
and, later, in film – became forbidden by the censor, evidently
out of fear that popular sentiment could be aroused by public
portrayals of the killing machine in favour of the abolition of
the death penalty, although in other media, such as illustrated
newspapers, picture postcards, carved models, and waxwork
tableaux, *la sainte guillotine* remained a great favourite throughout the nineteenth and early twentieth century, given various
affectionate nicknames, such as *la veuve, la bascule à Charlot,
l'abbaye de monte-à-regret*. Terror has its humour, its domesti-
cation, its attractions.[23]

Büchner's *Danton's Death* – the first important European
drama to deal with the French Revolution – was written in
1835 during a period of repression when the author, threatened with arrest for conspiratorial activities on behalf of the
German 'Society for the Rights of Man', was forced to go into
political exile. The play captures the nightmare atmosphere
of anxiety and dread that accompanies the Terror. 'Are we
not sleepwalkers?' Robespierre asks, unable to shake off
the dream state of loneliness and isolation that engulfs all
the characters. Büchner is transitional, looking as much back
to Shakespeare as forward to twentieth-century expressionism. In *Danton's Death*, the revolutionary mob continues Jack
Cade's anti-literacy crusade.

> THE FIRST CITIZEN: Death to anyone who can read
> and write! . . . we're the people. And our will is that
> there shouldn't be any law. *Ergo*, our will is law, *ergo*, in
> the name of the law there is no law. *Ergo*, death![24]

Büchner's technique is to unmask revolutionary ideology,
break open the façade, crack its skull, and see what is inside. A
playwright and medical student, Büchner finds only 'the hor-
rible fatalism of history' and the basic elements of man's nature
– sex, fear, hunger, weariness. 'The individual is only foam
upon the wave', and genius counts for nothing. It follows
from these gloomy premises that individualism must submit
to one single social will which can serve the community as a
whole. Out of his sense of helplessness, despair, and frustration, Büchner concludes, 'If in our age something is to help,

then it's violence.'[25] 'Each evening,' the author of *Danton's Death* admits, 'I pray for hemp and lanterns', looking back to the early pre-guillotine phase of the French Revolution when rope and lamp posts were used to string up enemies of the people.[25]

In Büchner's play, Danton's last words on the scaffold at the Place de la Révolution, spoken to the executioner who pushes back Herault as he tries to embrace his friend and fellow victim, 'Can you prevent our heads from kissing at the bottom of the basket?', are both a citation from the historical record and an apparent reference back to Cade's staging of the kissing heads. The final scenes of *Danton's Death* are dominated by the guillotine, about which men and women sing and dance the 'Carmagnole'; it is the 'Iron law' of history, against which only a ludicrous struggle can be waged. Like his hero, Danton, Büchner lost faith in the power of revolutionary action to effect fundamental change of a utopian kind, but he refused to acquiesce blindly in the irrational forces that had been let loose. The impasse was tragic.

3. *The Institutionalising of Terror: The Police State*

In Alexander Sukhovo-Kobylin's *The Case* (1861) and *The Death of Tarelkin* (1869), terror under tsarist despotism has become institutionalised within the cumbersome machinery of bureaucracy and police. According to the grotesque vision of the author (who spent seven nightmarish years in and out of Russian courts and jails on charges of murdering his mistress) the locus of terror is no longer the scaffold, but the police station where suspects are interrogated. The urge to arrest, on the assumption that everyone is a traitor engaged in anti-state conspiracies, reaches such proportions that madness threatens to engulf all of Russia. In a gloomy, dimly-lit police station, the setting of the last half of *The Death of Tarelkin*, loutish rogues in police uniforms conduct their investigations with the aid of broomsticks and a specially devised human beating machine constructed out of their moronic subordinates. Guilt by association is the fundamental principle of justice; innocent landowners and merchants are sent off to 'the secret chamber'; and terrified victims, bound to chairs and deprived of food and water, name as their accomplices, 'All Petersburg and all Moscow', readily confessing to being vampires and werewolves who have sucked the blood of their neighbours. The interrogators and torturers grow so enchanted with their work that they declare: 'Everything belongs to us now. "We'll demand all of Russia! . . . There aren't any people here – just monsters . . . All they deserve is Siberia and chains . . . That's why we have to establish a rule of subjecting everyone to arrest! . . . The machinery will operate by itself".'[27] Sukhovo-Kobylin's police-station state functions automatically; the terror has grown faceless, unfathomable, with no one in charge and no goal in mind beyond the blind perpetuation of the system.

4. *Ubu's Trap-door*

An extreme form of the modern terrorist state is forecast by Alfred Jarry's *Ubu Roi*. A caricature of Shakespearean models of usurping warlords and tyrannical monarchs, Père Ubu is a gross buffoon, a monstrous nonentity, a moronic bourgeois Tamburlaine. Instead of 'To the lamp post!' Ubu's terrorist slogan is 'Down the trap!'. Terror has descended from the raised scaffold to a hole in the ground; an anonymous death now awaits whole classes of people – Nobles, Magistrates, Financiers – who are quickly dispatched down the trap. The image is one of corpses being shovelled into a pit.

In *The Other Kingdom*, an account of life in the concentration camps, the French author David Rousset sees Ubu as the presiding spirit or tutelary deity of Buchenwald, Birkenau, Auschwitz, and Maidanek. Like the camps, Ubu's world is composed of utterly arbitrary, capricious and degrading elements: a toilet brush, a trapdoor, an endless procession of faceless victims to be liquidated for no reason at all. The disembraining machine is the Ubuesque modern medico-technological version of the guillotine, ready for use on friend and foe alike. Rousset points out that the worst human devastation was the castration of free brains effected by the camps, draining and emptying them by making the prisoners 'forge the instruments of their own annihilation'.[28] In the camps, the hangman's traditional arts were so perverted that perhaps even the ardent reactionary, Joseph de Maistre, would have been less convinced of the divine sanction for the executioner.

Because of Ubu, according to Rousset, it was possible for the concentration camp prisoners to make 'The fascinating discovery of humour, not so much as a projection of the personality, but as an objective pattern of the universe'. Drawing upon his reading of Shakespeare, his adolescent dislike for an authoritarian schoolmaster, and his intuitive grasp of the nature of political power as embodied in the contemptible rulers who would lead Europe into two world wars, Jarry created in Ubu a figure who represents 'everything that is grotesque in the world' and serves as a 'debased double' of the audience. Ubu is the incarnation of the banality of evil. In Jarry's *guignol* for adults we see how a crude nobody – the personification of bourgeois stupidity and mediocrity – can became an actor on the world-historical stage and determine the destiny of nations by robbing, plundering, and slaughtering. The 'terror of history' (as described by Mircea Eliade) has become a bloody farce.

5. *The End of Humanism*

World War I, the Russian Revolution, and the rise of dictatorships throughout Europe in the 1920s and 1930s brought the question of the terrorist ruler and the terrorist realm to the forefront of attention. Writers and intellectuals became fascinated with the terrorist phenomenon, and it is not surprising that a number of important plays on the subject appeared during the period between the wars. Among the most significant of these, for my purposes, are works by Witkiewicz, Jules Romains, Lagerkvist, Brecht, Stanisława Przybyszewska, Nordahl Grieg, Armand Salacrou, and Evgenii Shvarts, and in a moment I shall turn to them as illustrations of my argument.

The interplay between intellectuals and the terrorist state in the inter-war period is too complex and variable to be reduced to any formla. Sometimes there was outright endorsement and support, as Hannah Arendt has noted in *The Origins of Totalitarianism*, commenting on the 'remarkable fact that Hitler's and Stalin's widely publicised opinions about art and their persecutions of modern artists have never been able to destroy the attraction which the totalitarian movements have for avant-garde artists'.[29] In other instances, the response is more ambiguous. In an essay written shortly after the Revolution of 1917, 'The Collapse of Humanism', the poet and playwright Alexander Blok argued that the masses neither want nor need civilisation as it has previously existed. The time of humanism is past; a police state operating through the army and bureaucracy offers a more realistic way to govern. Identifying true culture with 'the element', the untutored people, the barbarian masses, Blok finds civilisation a crumbling façade ready to be swept away.[30] By the mid-1930s, the phenomenon of dictatorship, which had spread throughout most of Europe and become the dominant fact of political, social and cultural life in the inter-war years, was the subject of much commentary and not a little admiration on the part of certain artists and intellectuals. Writing in 1934, Paul Valéry observed that 'Dictatorship is at present contagious, just as, in the past, freedom was'.

6. The Terror of One Will as a Metaphysical Concept.

The Polish artist, playwright and philosopher, Stanisława Ignacy Witkiewicz, or Witkacy, for whom the French Revolution was the first major turning point in the decline of culture, shared Blok's apprehensive sense of the inevitable breakdown of elite civilisation and the demise of the individual, and at the same time anticipated Valéry's fascination with the philosophical bases for the imposition of uniformity upon the mass, of the will of the one upon the many.[31]

Witkacy is concerned with psychic terror, rather than with physical coercion through the economic, judicial, or military powers of the state. His terrorist realms are always utopian in intent. The aim is to return man to the unanimity and harmony of the ant-hill. In the words of the Russian religious philosopher, Nikolai Berdyaev, 'Utopia is always totalitarian.' A product of the 'Euclidian mind' (in Dostoevsky's phrase), utopia (Berdyaev explains) seeks to regulate all of life by reason and thus brings enforced happiness to mankind, at whatever cost.[31]

In *Gyubal Wahazar*, or *Along the Cliffs of the Absurd* (1921), subtitled 'A Non-Euclidian Drama in Four Acts', Witkacy projects the utopian idea into the future in accordance with the postulates of modern science. Happiness for all is forcibly instituted, not according to the familiar and predictable postulates of Euclidian geometry, but in accord with Einstein's theory of relativity, Cantor's theory of sets, Heisenberg's uncertainty principle, and Bohr's principle of complementarity. Witkacy portrays the totalitarian future as a world of indeterminacy and endless metamorphosis, a political realm 'with a six-dimensional continuum'. The sinister techniques of the new totalitarian statecraft are derived from a radically new view of human nature as something infinitely malleable, controllable, transmutable.

Whereas anti-utopian fantasies usually focus on the downtrodden victims of a repressive regime and depict their struggle to lead normal human lives – usually represented by romantic love – Witkacy centres *Gyubal Wahazar* on the dictator himself and his relation to his people. Instead of showing the terrorist state as a revolting aberration from the point of view of traditional humanistic values, the playwright enters imaginatively into the workings of dictatorship and dramatises the deep bonds between the oppressor and the oppressed which have their source in the changing demands of an evolving human nature. The time of humanism is over, as Blok had indicated. Future mankind no longer wants or needs freedom, but rather must be transformed into purposefully functioning insects in order to regain the mindless happiness known only to the members of the most primitive clans in prehistory. The insect analogy is as resonant for Witkacy as it was for the Čapek brothers, Bulgakov, Mayakovsky, and Orwell.

Valéry describes how the modern despot experiences delight in making an entire people carry out what a single person has ordained. In Witkacy's *Gyubal Wahazar*, we witness this process: the dictator's subjects become an extension of his thought, a part of him. Wahazar, known as His Onlyness, represents the higher function of the mind; the people are the raw human material, the automatic functions. The tyrant has reduced his subjects to the state of machine-made products. But the converse is also true; the despot is an extension of all those whom he has reduced to the level of objects, or of 'instruments of his thought'. The terrorist-tyrant does away with freedom, not only for others, but for himself as well. In encompassing all the objects who are his instruments, he has become no more than the sum of these parts and ultimately replaceable. 'All men have become One Man', Hannah Arendt explains in *The Origins of Totalitarianism*.[321] In *Gyubal Wahazar* the state scientist, Dr Rypman, conducts strange experiments involving 'the fission of psychic atoms' and will soon be able to fabricate new Wahazars out of hyenas, jackals, or even bedbugs. Thus his Onlyness, who has imagined that he is the sole deity, can be mechanically reproduced. Modern science and technology can be used to create a terrorist system that is self-perpetuating and self-proliferating, ready to take over the world.

When Witkacy first envisaged his bizarre terrorist realms, modern totalitarianism had scarcely come into being. For his portraits of totemic tyrants, the Polish playwright drew upon his discussions of cultural anthropology with Bronislaw Malinowski, his reading of Shakespeare and of *Ubu Roi*, his knowledge of the French Revolution, his experiences in Russia before, during, and after 1917, and his own battles with a domineering artist-father who terrorised his son by insisting that he always be free and creative. In *They*, a play in two-and-a-half acts, Witkacy evokes the feelings of paranoia that come from living in constant dread of a masked power structure whose identity and operation are unknowable. 'They' – ubiquitous and protean – have seized control of our lives and enforce the tyranny of society over the individal. A secret government is located deep within the visible government; weird committees and agencies are at work planning the regimentation of thought and feeling.

The terrorism unleashed at the end of Witkacy's plays comes as a nasty *coup de théâtre*, all the more menacing because arbitrary and unpredictable; its origins, ideology, and sources of power are not easily identifiable and cannot be reduced to any single political party or platform. It seems a mixture of the extreme left and the extreme right. All we know is that it is collective terror – less systematic than spontaneous – of the mass against the individual. Secrecy characterises its organisation, and joy-in-destruction is its motive force. The victims find in their very doom the only possible justification for ever having lived and readily accept their own suffering and extinction, even, inventing pretexts to hasten the retribution. Subject to mental coercion and surrounded by informers even in his own home, the weak intellectual hero of *They* sees his precious art collection destroyed by the League of Absolute Automation and is made to feel such guilt that he confesses to a crime that he has not committed.

The Anonymous Work, 'Four Acts of a Rather Nasty Nightmare' (1921), is a Witkacian version of *Hamlet* in which the Gravediggers replace the Prince. Undertakers of a dying world and midwives of an emerging one, the two Gravediggers are out to bury their masters. A revolution occurs within a revolution, as the rabble seizes power from its leaders. The pseudo-theocratic revolution based on a pseudo-ideology is taken over by the lowest elements, who fashion 'The Anonymous Work' – the true terrorist revolution. The faceless mob, acting on unconscious impulses, sweeps away all barriers; it succeeds because it sinks to the lowest level and espouses mass destruction. Violence triumphs as ideology is buried. Under the leadership of the Gravedigger, Lopak, the mob of levellers (not unlike Jack Cade's troops) scream, 'On to the palace! Hang the whole government!'. The former leaders of the first, pseudo-theocratic *coup d'état* are strung up on an improvised scaffold. 'To the lamppost!' is the cry, echoing down the corridor of history from the time of the French Revolution. 'Down with the personality! Long live the uniform MASS, one and indivisible!!!!'[33]

7. *Them or Us!*

In 1920 the Civil War in the USSR was at its most critical stage; internal enemies, abetted by foreign intervention, were threatening the existence of the new Bolshevik regime. In Soviet-occupied territories, terror became an acknowledged means of government. In *Year One of the Russian Revolution*, Victor Serge justifies the terror on a variety of grounds: there was no alternative but to destroy or be destroyed; to organise terror means to limit it; no revolution ever happened without terror; the propertied classes always use terror; there were no innocents among the bourgeoisie; the Red Terror was less bloody than the White Terror; fewer people were killed throughout the Civil War by terror than were shot in Paris in one week by the Versailles troops during the liquidation of the Commune or killed on a single day during the battle of Verdun.

A further argument advanced by the Bolsheviks for the Terror was the analogy between their revolution and the great French Revolution. The men and women of 1917 saw themselves as repeating the events and re-enacting the characters of 1789. 'These September days', Serge writes, 'so reminiscent of their parallel in the French Revolution, mark like their predecessor – and for similar reasons – the inauguration of the era of terror.'[34] As in the French Revolution, the terror was not only a necessary weapon in the class war, but also a terrible instrument for the inner purification of the proletarian dictatorship – in other words, for removing rivals and getting rid of any one regarded as potentially dangerous. But, unlike the festive public guillotinings in Paris, the Bolshevik terror was carried out in 'virtually total secrecy', without admitting the right to defence, without even hearing the accused. Executions took place quickly and quietly in cellars, by revolver, to avoid arousing untoward emotions.

In the second version of Vladimir Mayakovsky's *Mystery-Bouffe*, staged by Vsevolod Meyerhold in May, 1921, the concrete political situation of the time is directly invoked, and ruthless vengeance against class enemies is nonchalantly instigated. In the name of the workers, 'the uniform, grey, sticky, stinking, monstrous mass' that Witkacy had depicted with fascinated horror in *The Anonymous Work*, the Russian Futurist poet justifies violence in exterminating counter-revolutionary opposition.

THE UNCLEAN: It's either them or us!
FARMHAND: Make way for the reign of terror!
BLACKSMITH: Sure, comrades,
Kick the weaklings over the side![35]

In the long speech by the Man, who appears walking on the waters (played by Mayakovsky) the new anti-beatitudes include a rejection of meekness and forgiveness in favour of aggression. Terror is such a natural and necessary weapon in the context of the Civil War that it needs no apology or explanation.

8. *Propaganda as terrorism; terrorism as propaganda*

Under the seemingly engaging and harmless guise of traditional French farce, Jules Romains wrote in 1923 what is perhaps the most universal and richly allusive of all modern plays about state terror: *Dr Knock, or the Triumph of Medicine*. Long interested in the cohesion of social groups as a result of his theory and practice of *unanisme* (or *unanimisme*), Romains shared Witkacy's philosophic concern with the imposition of one will upon the many and was fascinated by the concept of the dictatorial ruler. But whereas Witkacy feared the process of de-individuation, Romains celebrated the fusion of individuals into collectives through the contagion of ideas. *Dr Knock* explores the formation of a suprapersonal consciousness through a universal cult with its own special rituals, of which Dr Knock is the high priest. The hero preys on human weaknesses and fears, using medical terror to transform a sleepy town made up of isolated individuals into parts of a smoothly functioning machine. As medical consumers, they find that their lives have been given purpose; by being regimented into a whole, they feel that they belong to something larger than themselves. By the end of the play the inhabitants of the formerly old-fashioned village have become efficient members of a new twentieth-century medical existence, all parts of one collective enterprise.

Dr Knock is one of the truly prophetic plays of the inter-war years. By its very simplicity, the tale expands into a parable of all modern societies. Romains's play is not only a brilliant forecast of contemporary medical history, in which improved technologies create needs and maintain a system of submission to authority, but it is also by extension an analysis of the operation of the entire corporate state, whether capitalist or socialist, and its control of each of its citizens. By his mastery of modern techniques of propaganda and indoctrination, Dr Knock is able to terrorise an entire community and make it submissive to his will. But he does everything for the good of his patients by making them realise that a healthy person is only a sick person who is not aware that he is

sick. Dr Knock's utopia, medical existence (and it could as
easily be capitalist existence or socialist existence), is totalitarian, as Berdyaev claimed utopia always is. Dr Knock's
terrorism is based on fear and threats of death; devoid
of overt violence it is a more insidious domination of the
mind.

Romains admires in Dr Knock the creative spirit that
transforms disparate individuals into a new collective entity.
Whether he is a fraud or a genius, we can never discover. Dr
Knock wears an impenetrable mask of solemnity, realising
that the greatest threat to his imposition of the medical existence is laughter; he has won his battle when he frightens the
two local wise guys and takes away their desire to laugh: submission now is total. We, as audience, laugh, but at whom?
Dr Knock's medical terrorism brings into being a modern
world that is perfectly organised and functional, but antiseptic
and sterile, a cautionary utopian construction, not unlike the
world of the future in Zamyatin's *We* and Mayakovsky's *The
Bedbug*.

9. 'Long live the killers!' – A history of the executioner

In *The Hangman* (1933), Pär Lagerkvist contrasts traditional
terror with modern Fascist terrorism by means of a brief history of the executioner through the ages. In the first half of the
play, set in a tavern in the Middle Ages, the executioner is a
figure apart, held in awe, outside the human community, yet
well known to it.

The human attraction to evil and violence is both presented
and held partially in check by the figure of the executioner. In
a cruel, violent fallen world, conscious of its own sinfulness
and ruled by superstition (which proves to be less destructive
than political ideology), terror is contained within the traditional structures of religion and society, however arbitrary and
unjust these may be. In *The Hangman*, the people even find that
'Evil has a healing power' when it is part of an entire world
of belief. The counter-revolutionary Joseph de Maistre claims
that the executioner is the very basis of civilisation: 'All grandeur, all power, all subordination rests on the executioner:
he is the horror and the bond of human association. Remove
this incomprehensible agent from the world, and at that very

moment order gives way to chaos, thrones topple, and society disappears'.[36]

In the second section of Lagerkvist's play, which takes place in a nightclub in the early 1930s, the worship of evil unrestrained by superstition has become an open celebration of violence. The Hangman himself has been made a god – rather than an executioner of God's will, as he was before. The ideological goal (which starts with the indoctrination of children) is to purify humanity of all who are different. The mania for oneness and unanimity means that all who think differently must be exterminated, and there are now many people to be liquidated. Universal hatred is let loose; impersonal violence becomes an end in itself.

Lagerkvist's analysis goes beyond a class or economic explanation of the rise of Fascist terror (such as is given in Brecht's *Arturo Ui*). The Swedish author explores human fascination with evil and the rituals of terror, the relation of sexuality and violence, and the sadistic appeals to racial hatred, all of which cut across class and economic boundaries. As one of the Fascist revellers at the nightclub declares, 'There are no more classes any more.' The erotic and racial aspects of terrorism, which the Nazis knew so well how to exploit, lie deep within the human psyche and serve to explain the attraction of Fascism in Germany on such a vast scale among all classes.

Once the executioner becomes the object of hypnotic mass worship, all the bonds of human society disintegrate – quite the opposite of what de Maistre feared. By setting both sections of *The Hangman* in communal places of drinking and entertainment, Lagerkvist depicts terror as a public spectacle whose theatrical impact is overwhelming. In Fascist society, the demarcations between the executioner and the people disappear. The mob becomes over-familiar with the hangman and ultimately take over his functions. A soldier attacks the Hangman as inefficient, saying, 'he ought to use machine guns'.[37] As several assassins enter the nightclub, the crowd cries out, 'Hail to the murderers!'.[38]

In the short epilogue at Golgotha offering a timeless, metaphysical vista, we have the Hangman's own apologia. The executioner, elder brother of Jesus, is a martyr who has taken man's guilt and violence on his own shoulders. He explains to humans, 'I am your Christ'.[39] Where belief has declined in the saving powers of a degenerate religion, a dead god, and a failed and feeble saviour, all that remains is corrupt human nature and the hangman.

10. *History through the lens of history: 1789 and 1871 seen from 1917*

After 1917, guided by the experiences of the Russian Revolution, a number of playwrights on the left reinterpreted the French Revolution and the Paris Commune. In the light of the events in Russia, they re-examined the use of terror to defend the revolution.

In her historical dramas, *The Danton Case* (1929) and *Thermidor* (1925), the Polish playwright, Stanisława Przybyszewska, was the first significant European playwright to view the French Revolution from the perspective of 1917. Drawing upon the revisionist historian, Albert Mathiez, she rehabilitated the terrorist Robespierre, who until then had been made the scapegoat for all the crimes and excesses of the Revolution. For Przybyszewska, a reading of the French Revolution in the light of recent Bolshevik history served not as a justification for the terror, but rather as a warning of the course that events in the Soviet Union would undoubtedly take. The analogy between contemporary happenings in Russia and those in Paris at the end of the eighteenth century revealed 'the radical evil of the revolutionary mechanism'.

The tragedy of all revolutions, the Polish author argued, is that there comes a certain moment when the whole undertaking must be centralised around a single leader. After a mortal struggle between rivals, concentration of power in the hands of one man is inevitable. Only by assuming dictatorial powers can the Incorruptible save the Republic, but in so doing he will destroy the freedom he seeks to preserve. Then the man of action, the relentless technocrat, Napoleon – *tyrannus triumphans* – will usurp power and use for his own selfish ends what the speculative, Enlightenment ideologue, Robespierre, had conceived as a great collective enterprise for all mankind. 'The thought, the will, the energy of a single human brain has to penetrate the entire society and decide its every movement', Przybyszewska declares, voicing the same conception of totalitarianism as Valéry, but seeing it as the fatal consequence of the revolutionary mechanism which can only bring tyranny and disaster.

According to Przybyszewska, *The Danton Case* treats politics in a fashion beyond politics, that is, without taking sides or promoting any ideological position. For the first time the Polish playwright renders human and believable, although not necessarily likable, the most mysterious and misunderstood figure of the revolution, Robespierre. Whereas Büchner has depicted a volcanic but essentially passive Danton, staggering under the burden of mortality while engaged in an unequal battle with an abstract, rigid Robespierre, Przybyszewska shifts the focus and portrays the Incorruptible as a brilliant, highly principled statesman confronted by political decisions and their consequences, as he faces the impossible task of governing France on the verge of chaos and preserving the new Republic from the attacks of powerful enemies, within and without. Chief of these enemies is the crafty, unscrupulous Danton. 'The terror is ruled only by *despair*.'[40] Robespierre admits, wishing to avoid executing the traitor Danton, knowing that such a desperate action will only swell the ranks of counter-revolution. 'The Danton case is a dilemma. If we lose, the whole Revolution is as good as lost. And if we win . . . the same is probably true.'[41]

Instead of the flamboyant gestures and heightened pathos of the spectacular dénouement of *Danton's Death*, with its scaffold, guillotine, and executioners (as Lucille Desmoulins seeks to join her husband in death by defiantly crying out, 'Long live the king!', which is historically inaccurate), Przybyszewska in her characteristic objective and controlled manner presents a quiet, brooding scene in which Robespierre, alone in his monastic room with his acolyte Saint-Just, recognises that by institutionalising the Terror, he has brought about the end of the Revolution; he predicts his own downfall and the rise of a dictatorship based on nationalism, militarism, and greed. 'The future belongs to the late Danton',[42] the Incorruptible observes ironically. 'The gangster-morality of a Danton or Napoleon will triumph. Robespierre will have to be eliminated so that the nineteenth century – mercenary, corrupt, and bloody – can come into being, and after it, our own monstrous age with its

nationalism, imperialist wars, and horrors.' The Terror that the
gentle, introspective Robespierre hoped to control in the name
of the despotism of virtue instead led directly to twentieth-
century totalitarianism and the decline of all revolutionary
ideals. Such is the tragic mechanism of revolution, according
to Stanisława Przybyszewska.

11. *The Paris Commune—next time, more terror*

Nordahl Grieg in *The Defeat* and Bertolt Brecht in *The Days
of the Commune*, a *Gegenstück*, or critical response, inspired by
Grieg's play, are partisan in their commitment to the ideals of
the Commune, but critical of its failure from an excess of good
will and faith in ideals. The triumph of the Bolshevik Revolution demonstrated exactly what should have been done.
The leaders of the Commune were insufficiently ruthless in
their application of Terror to crush counter-revolutionary class
enemies. The basic lesson of the Commune was the need
for dictatorial authority, Red Terror, and aggressive military
initiative. Trotsky explained that the Paris Commune's commitment to 'democratic legality' was the cause of its undoing;
'sentimental humaneness' and 'generosity' towards its enemies led to the ultimate slaughter during the Bloody Week
in May, when the Commune's opponents had no qualms
about murdering thousands. Of the Soviet Terror during the
Civil War, Trotsky declared, 'We are taking vengeance for the
Commune and we shall avenge it'. Both dedicated to the Communist cause, Grieg and Brecht followed this line of analysis
in their theatrical portrayals of the Commune although in very
different ways and with radically different results.

The Paris Commune – for a brief sixty-five days the first
proletarian revolution – was a subject off limits for drama
in France for almost a century, at first because of political
censorship lasting until 1905 and then because of the prevailing social and political atmosphere that made the Commune
taboo. There were, of course, some plays written on the subject, but those that got produced (mainly by Antoine at the
Théâtre Libre in the late 1880s and 1890s) were necessarily
timid attempts to arouse sympathy for the pathetic Commu-
nards who had been vanquished and banished for defending
a misguided lost cause. All the best-known writers of the

period were anti-Communard, and official culture ignored or repudiated the events of 1871. In the theatre in France no one wrote openly in praise of the virtues of the Commune until Adamov's *Printemps 71* in 1960 and the great outpouring of French plays on the subject came only after the 1968 revolution, which sought to re-enact the Days of the Commune.

But in Russia after 1917 the situation had become quite the opposite. Hundreds of Commune plays were written and performed, in the twenties, celebrating its way of life and egalitarian values, praising it as the beginning of the World Revolution, and linking it directly to the Bolshevik Revolution, which brought to successful completion what the men and women of 1871 had begun. Often written by amateurs as contest entries for festive performances at clubs and factories or in army units on March 18, the day of the establishment of the Paris Commune and a Soviet holiday, these plays celebrated the heroic, joyous, internationalist aspects of the Commune through the non-traditional forms of agit drama, mass spectacles, trials, rewritten operas, Blue Blouse acrobatics, living newspapers, and recitations. Like the Commune itself, these were participatory collective dramas about the group, glorifying not the leaders, but the masses, *la canaille*. This grass-roots, self-starting theatrical movement showed the Commune not as defeated, but as prefiguring 1917 and the experiences of the present in Russia – a joining of hands between the living and the dead. These were indeed 'the anonymous work', part of a vast theatre mania throughout USSR that prospered for nearly ten years until, starting in 1928, it was suppressed by Stalinist centralisation and control of the arts with its elimination of all that was local and spontaneous and by the imposition of the standardised aesthetic norms of socialist realism.

Out of this mass of topical and occasional Russian Commune plays comes the freeing of the subject for the theatre. The dramas of Grieg and Brecht grow out of this soil. *The Defeat* (1937), the richest play on the Commune and the most probing treatment of the problem of Red Terror, was written in 1937 after Grieg's visit to the USSR and in the shadow of the Spanish Civil War. The growing success of Fascism in Europe made the lessons of the Commune all the more evident: it was necessary to strike first, to destroy the enemies of the revolution. Nordahl Grieg was a man of action, a militant whose commitment to Communism was romantic and impulsive. A believer in making choices and taking risks, he had become a sailor at nineteen, travelled to China in 1927 when the Civil War was raging, and gone to Moscow in 1933–34, where he became a friend of Meyerhold and Boris Pilnyak and a devoted Stalinist (who would defend the purge trials). He had visited Spain in 1936, joined the Norwegian resistance in 1940, and was killed with the RAF in a raid over Berlin in 1943.

Despite Grieg's total personal commitment, *The Defeat* stresses the tragic dilemma inherent in revolutionary causes that must be fought for using the unworthy means of the enemy and that, to be preserved, entail sacrifices that make them no longer worth preserving. In other words, what made the Commune so precious as a joyous, spontaneous expression of the will to live and love as free men and women doomed it to failure. The Commune was a singing revolution, but revolutions are not won by song. To save the Commune what was needed was vengeance, terror, and aggressive and self-disciplined militarism in attacking the Versailles forces – in other words, all the traditional warlike masculine qualities that Przybyszewska in *The Danton Case* had shown as leading to dictatorship and the collapse of revolutionary ideals. In *The Defeat*, Grieg's analysis is carried out not as Przybyszewska's was, among the leadership exclusively, but rather, among a wide spectrum of all the people involved.

Grieg dramatises the many different and conflicting positions held by the participants in the struggle, opposing one to another in a series of dialectical clashes that remain unresolved and unresolvable. Humanism, decency, belief in love and creativity are contrasted with the need for terror, violence, and the destruction of the old order. General Rossel's despairing complaint that he cannot win the battle for the Commune without disciplined troops is countered by a Communard's insistence on enjoying his freedom now and not in some distant future. If the people cannot have the sensuous immediacy of loving, eating, and drinking, why should they fight?

In *The Defeat* Grieg creates numerous memorable portraits

including those of the honest idealistic artisan Varlin, the cunning Marquis de Ploeuc, Vice Governor of the Bank, and the narcissistic revolutionary artist, Gustave Courbet, but none are more powerful than those of the young revolutionary terrorist, Raoul Rigault, and his counterpart at the other end of the spectrum, the eighty-year-old state terrorist, Adolphe Thiers. At opposite extremes, these two advocates of terror are alike in being cold, ruthless, impersonal, standing alone without human ties, absolute in their ideological consistency. Each is sexually pure – Thiers in his ascetic, sterile impotence, Rigault in his emotionless debauchery. They both despise life, a hatred which gives them their strength.

Grieg makes the picture of the revolutionary terrorist as logically compelling and terrifying as possible. A young medical student thrown out of school for his radical views, a high-living frequenter of bars and brothels, Rigault became Chief of Police and then public Prosecutor under the Commune. An advocate of the shooting of hostages, he was dead at twenty-five, shot by the Versailles troops. He has always been the *bête noire* of the Commune, unacceptable even to its proponents, but Grieg presents his arguments in a persuasive form. Rigault explains to the horrified Varlin, just before ordering the shooting of the prisoners:

> Ten thousand lives might have been saved if I had been allowed to paralyse Versailles with terror. Look at what your love of mankind has led to, you drivelling hangman! [*Yells*] Shoot them down to the last man!
>
> There fell the Archbishop! If I haven't done another good act in the world, at least I have done this. I have shown that we can liquidate an archbishop just as unconcernedly as Versailles kills a worker. People have one less superstition to carry.
>
> I dare use my intelligence, I reserve the right to distinguish between purposeful extermination and stupid.[43]

In the scene with the Governor of the Bank (which Brecht imitated), Grieg shows how easy it is for the honest old worker Beslay to be tricked into respecting the sanctity of the gold of France (used by Thiers to finance the suppression of the Commune). Even more powerful than the Terror is the control of money, the Governor declares to the emissary from Versailles. The artisan Beslay has the ideals of little people: 'thrift and honesty'. 'He calls himself a socialist, but he lacks the imagination necessary to overthrow a society', the Governor explains. 'I feel that the existing society has an invincible companion: the socialists' own fear of socialism.' From this perspective, even Rigault is engaged in 'his comparatively harmless activity of organising terror and arresting hostages.'[44] The only 'real hostages' are 'the gold ingots in the Bank of France.'[45]

Brecht wrote *The Days of the Commune* in 1948–49 in Zurich after reading Grieg's play. We know that Brecht admired *The Defeat*; in 1949 he recommended it to Piscator and then planned to adapt it himself. But *The Days of the Commune* is an original play that contains only a few characters and features taken from Grieg; it is, Brecht says, intended rather as a counter to *The Defeat*. His last full-length play, it was to be the first original production at the Berliner Ensemble.

It is easy to understand why Brecht would have rejected Grieg's essentially tragic vision of the Commune, its portrayal of the fear and loneliness of its heroes and heroines facing death for a lost cause, its overwhelming sense of emotional turmoil and catastrophe, and its ambiguous portrayal of the one man who knows how to save the revolution, the ruthless, daring terrorist, Rigault. In Brecht's answer to Grieg, the focus narrows upon the leadership's failure to understand the correct revolutionary strategy. Seen in the perspective of the successful Russian Revolution and the establishment of Communist governments in East Germany and throughout Eastern Europe, the defeat of the Commune is only temporary. The positive characters in *The Days of the Commune* develop a growing awareness of the need to fight back, and although they learn too late, the lesson is absorbed by history. Whereas Grieg's play abounds in anguished contradictions, Brecht's *Days of the Commune* is largely affirmative. The choices are binary: fight back or be destroyed. To burn the guillotine publicly, but fail to seize possession of the bank, is suicidal.

Without whores, brandy, or expensive cigarettes, Brecht's Rigault has been sanitised and reduced to a rather colourless spokesman for the correct ideological position of resistance: 'Terror for terror: oppress or you'll be oppressed. Crush or

they'll crush you.' 'I am asking only for terror to fight terror.'[46]
Gone is any frightening extremism in the portrait of Rigault
that could make him seem a mirror image of Thiers, or any
of the sexual sadism that accompanies the terror on both
sides in Grieg's *Defeat*. Brecht's Rigault is a kind of *raisonneur*
arguing for the power of the people and their need to intervene directly outside the constraints of bourgeois legality and
morality: the error was in failing to take military action and
march on Versailles. In *The Days of the Commune* the word *terror*
is used sparingly and discretely, only as a countermeasure in
response to the state terrorism of Thiers.

Grieg's Rigault, on the other hand, exults in terror as a
universal principle of revolution:

> Bourgeois society accepts *war*, the blind, confused anni-
> hilation of unknown destinies. But terror – the logical
> destruction of definite enemies – is regarded with horror.
> Why? Because human beings do not dare acknowledge
> their own nature; when they murder, they want to mur-
> der in the dark. But I will murder in the full daylight of my
> reason. . . . Strong, annihilating violence creates peace.
> . . . *All new life is born in blood*.[47]

12. *Children as Terrorists*

Witkacy dealt extensively with pseudo-theocratic forms of
terrorism. The secular religions of the modern totalitarian
state, communism and fascism, have their own fanaticism
that results in special forms of terror that delight in degrading
and humiliating one's elders. In Salacrou's *The World Is Round*,
set in fifteenth-century Florence, wandering bands of youths,
disciples of Savonarola, go about from house to house, repeating their formulas, 'Christ is king' and 'Brother Jerome is the
protector of the Republic', ripping up books and smashing art
objects, while at the same time insulting adults – sometimes
their own parents or relatives – as 'fat bourgeois' or 'great fat
pig', and then sending them to be whipped. The generational
vengeance and the pleasure in the sadistic tearing-down of
adult authority that Salacrou depicts had its direct analogue in
the events that were taking place in Germany in 1937, but the
rampage of fanatical young people attacking culture found its
fullest counterpart in reality in the terror spread throughout

China by the Red Guard during the Cultural Revolution of the
1960s and 70s.

13. *Terror as a collaborative enterprise*

In his fairy-tale plays for adults *The Naked King*, *The Shadow*,
and *The Dragon*, the Soviet children's author Evgenii Shvarts
explores the collaborative nature of the terrorist state – in other
words, the everydayness of terror as seen from the inside by
those who are both its victims and its support, who tolerate
it, suffer under it, and profit from it. Shvarts asks, why do
people capitulate, how as a collective social body do they
learn to accept servitude, venality, and compromise? For
the terrorist repressive regime to exist, people must acquiesce
and become co-creators. In *The Dragon*, the dragon system is
shown to be so deeply rooted, the evil so ingrained, the seeds
of submission so lodged within us, that it can survive reform
and change of regime. The open, paternalistic dictatorship of
the dragon is over thrown only to be replaced by a more modern, hypocritical system of oppression, camouflaged under a
democratic façade. The apathy induced by the terrorist state
causes widespread resistance to change and a clinging to
tyranny. To the enslaved, only honesty is terrifying, posing,
as it does, a threat to corruption. It requires constant effort to
be free.

'The saddest thing in the whole story is that they smile,'
says the Cat, commenting on the lying and hypocrisy endemic
to the Dragon's realm. Shvarts examines the effects of terror
on language with a sharp ear for the absurd. Not only is all
public information distorted (as in the official accounts of the
Dragon's battles with Lancelot), but also in private life the
constant need to dissemble results in a kind of double-talk.
The extent and ease of adaptation to the system is appalling.
The very familiarity of the Dragon causes normal people to
rationalise and justify the terror. One's own Dragon is pre-
ferable to an unknown foreign one; our Dragon has been a
good protector after all, he eliminated the Gypsies. Shvarts's
The Dragon remains relatively optimistic in suggesting that
eternal vigilance and a willingness to combat stupidity, con-
formity, and passivity may suffice to eradicate the dragon.

The Shadow is a bleaker study of the corrupting effects of terror on its victims, who, in turn, become its co-creators. In this slightly earlier play, written on the eve of the Second World War, the playwright looks at the dark, buried side of human nature that lies at the centre of the world of terror. It is a nightmarish world of dreams and shadows, of dissolving images and menacing doubles. The cannibalisation of mankind takes place because of the acquiescence of victims whose most chilling defence against the horrors around them are indifference, cynicism and irony. In the realm of *The Shadow*, where false appearance and total distrust reign, no one can be innocent, and it is dangerous to converse with strangers. The menace of terrorism is everywhere, Shvarts makes clear, in human passivity and compliance – it is our shadow, our double, from which we can never be completely free. 'The block has been placed in the pink salon, near the statue of Cupid, and it's hidden beneath forget-me-nots.'

Flowers covering the executioner's block; it is at this point that I shall break off my account of the conjunction of civilisation and terror in European drama from the Elizabethans to the interwar avante-garde. We know only too well that thereafter the history of state terror simply begins a new chapter. Playwrights such as Ionesco, Dürrenmatt, Örkény, Mrożek, and Havel have continued to explore in new dramaturgical modes the oppression of the individual at the hands of the state. The subject is still very much alive. If the counter-terrorism of the individual against the state sometimes seems to attract more attention, it is because isolated acts of violence create stories of obvious human interest, involving personal reactions and motivations, which are perfectly suited to exploitation in the mass media. But drama is by its very essence a collective, social form that can best attack the problem of the intimidation of the few by the many. In *The Second Year of Liberty* (1988), a new play about the French Revolution by the Soviet writer, Alexander Buravsky, the powerful theatrical image of the guillotine decked in flowers reveals how terror can cloak itself in noble revolutionary ideals and stirring artistic slogans. The line of drama that I have been discussing has not yet reached an end.

NOTES

1. Max Horkheimer and Theodor Adorno, *Dialectic of Enlightenment*, trans. John Cumming (New York: Herder and Herder, 1972), 217.
2. Paul Wilkinson, *Political Terrorism* (New York: John Wiley & Sons, 1974), 36-44.
3. Lacey Baldwin Smith, *Treason in Tudor England: Politics and Paranoia* (Princeton: Princeton University Press, 1986), 161, 163.
4. Ibid., 65, 78, 82.
5. Lacey Baldwin Smith, 'English Treason Trials and Confessions in the Sixteenth Century' in *The Elizabethan Age*, ed. David L. Stevenson (Greenwich, Conn: Fawcett, 1967).
6. Albert Camus, *The Rebel*, trans. Anthony Bower (New York: Vintage, 1958), 177-80.
7. Clifford Leech, *Christopher Marlowe: Poet for the Stage* (New York: AMS Press, 1986), 170.
8. *Henry VI*, Part II, 4, 2: in *The Complete Works of William Shakespeare* (London: Octopus Press. 1982), 535.
9. Ronald Paulson, *Representations of Revolution (1789-1820)* (New Haven: Yale, 1983), 21.
10. *Henry VI*, Part II, 4, 8, 539; 5, 2, 544.
11. Ibid., 4, 2, 537.
12. Ibid., 4, 7, 539.
13. Elie Halevy, *The Era of Tyrannies*, trans. R. K. Webb (New York: New York University, 1966), 266.
14. *Richard III*, 3, 5-6, 594.
15. Gerald Gould, 'Irony and Satire in *Henry V*' in *Shakespeare: Henry V: A Casebook* (Nashville: Aurora, 1970), 81.
16. Smith, *Treason In Tudor England*, 164.
17. Jean Starobinski, *1789: The Emblems of Reason*, trans. Denise Elliot and Jackson Matthews (New York: Pantheon, 1962), 5.
18. John Wilson Croker, *Essays on the Early Period of the French Revolution*, (New York: AMS Press, 1970), 553-4.
19. Ibid., 528.
20. Lynn Hunt, *Politics, Culture and Class in the French Revolution* (Berkeley: University of California, 1982), 46.
21. Christopher Hibbert, *The Days of the French Revolution* (New York: Morrow Quill, 1981), 274.
22. Croker, op. cit., 569.
23. Alain Monestier, ed., *Le Fait divers* (Paris: Edition de la Réunion des musées nationaux, 1982), 42-9.
24. Georg Büchner, *Danton's Death* in *The Plays of Georg Büchner*, trans. Victor Price (Oxford: Oxford University Press, 1971), 10-11.

25. William C. Reeve, *Georg Büchner* (New York: Ungar, 1979, 12.
26. Ibid., 10.
27. *The Trilogy*, trans. Harold B. Segel (New York: Dutton, 1969), 243, 260, 244, 243. 253.
28. David Rousset, *The Other Kingdom*, trans. Ramon Guthrie (New York: Reynal and Hitchcock, 1947), 111, 165-6.
29. *The Origins of Totalitarianism* (Cleveland: Meridian, 1967), 355.
30. Avril Pyman, *The Life of Aleksandr Blok*, Vol. II, *The Release of Harmony* 1920-1921 (Oxford: Oxford University Press, 1980), 333-40.
31. Robert C. Elliott, *The Shape of Utopia: Studies in a Literary Genre* (Chicago: University of Chicago Press, 1970), 90-1.
32. Arendt, op. cit., 477.
33. *Year One of the Russian Revolution*, trans and ed. Peter Sedgewick (Chicago: Holt, Rhinehart and Winston, 1972), 290.
34. *The Anonymous Work* in *Twentieth-Century Polish Avant-Garde Drama*, ed. Daniel Gerould (Ithaca: Cornell, 1977), 150, 149.
35. *Mystery-Bouffe* in Vladimir Mayakovsky, *The Complete Plays of Vladimir Mayakovsky*, trans. Guy Daniels (New York: Simon and Shuster, 1971), 81-2.
36. Joseph de Maistre, *Works*, selected and translated by Jack Lively (New York: Macmillan, 1965), 192.
37. *The Hangman* in Pär Lagerkvist, *Modern Theatre: Seven Plays and an Essay*, trans. Thomas R. Buckman (Lincoln: University of Nebraska, 1966), 186.
38. Ibid., 189.
39. Ibid., 202.
40. *The Danton Case* in *The Danton Case: Thermidor – Two Plays*, trans. Boleslaw Taborski (Evanston: Northwestern University, 1989), 59.
41. Ibid., 155.
42. Ibid., 209.
43. *The Defeat*, trans. J. B. C. Watkins in *Modern Scandanavian Theatre*, ed. Robert W. Corrigan (New York: Macmillan 1967), 389.
44. Ibid., 360.
45. Ibid., 361.
46. *The Days of the Commune*, trans. Chris Bahr and Arno Reinfrank (London: Eyre Methuen, 1978), 74.
47. *The Defeat*, 356-7.

2

Terrorism as Social Drama and Dramatic Form

JOHN ORR

I

The classic definition of terror comes from Aristotle's *Poetics*. In classical tragedy, terror (*phobos*) is unleashed along with pity by the demise of the hero in cathartic scenes of catastrophe and death. Enlarging Aristotle's definition, the young James Joyce wrote, 'Terror is the feeling which arrests us before whatever is grave in human fortunes and unites us with its secret cause.' He had previously called 'improper' in either comedy or tragedy, the feelings of loathing and desire, loathing being 'the feeling which urges us to go from something' while 'terror and pity hold us in rest, as it were, by fascination'.[1] There can be no doubt of the continuing fascination of terror. Its offshoot, modern terrorism, is often seen as originating in the actions of the Jacobins during the French revolution. The Reign of Terror was a systematic intimidation of others, based upon ideological foundations, that moved people to act through fear of what had already happened to the victims of that terror. We often see terrorism as systematic terror, whose violence towards the innocent we feel to be loathsome. Yet aesthetically, tragic terror holds us in rest through fascination. How do we reconcile the two? Is there not a fascination in the feelings terror excites? Does not the 'Stockholm Syndrome' suggest that after an intense period of capitivity hostages will feel grateful to their kidnappers? Can terrorism then be seen only as a source of loathing?

The answer, of course, is that it cannot, and that the fascination cannot be dismissed as pathological. For terrorism

48

uses violence as a gruesome theatre of the unexpected whose performers are anonymous. It is a theatre of paradox. It openly seeks publicity through actions whose origins it wishes to keep a closely-guarded secret. We do not know where it will strike, but where it does it looks for headlines, outrage. bewilderment and fear. Like the Committee of Public Safety, it seeks to destroy the illusion of public safety. Its methods are thus highly performative. In order for its political ends to have some impact, if not success, it must also be a form of social drama, a presentation of abnormality in everyday life. Through a combination of conspiracy and social drama, terrorists exert a secret power which atones for their lack of official power. The question we have to answer is how such social dramas work and who originates them.

Rubenstein's important study of contemporary terrorism suggests two important things. Terrorism against the state is largely originated by young intellectuals who have lost faith in their power to 'move' their audience through conventional forms of communication, while its specific modernity lies in its acceptance of basic forms of technical rationality, experimentation and control.[2] We are no longer in the romantic age of anarchist terrorism to which Camus referred in *L'Homme révolté*. Terrorism is a permanent feature of modernity in the age of the AK-47 assault rifle and the radio-controlled 'device'. And it is global, crossing frontiers at will. It may have no real home, no true resting-place, but it has many hiding-places. It does not live, conveniently, in one country or one society. It does not belong to a bounded world.

Ranged against it are the more complex and powerful agencies of state terror. These are under some constitutional limitations in the liberal regimes of the West but in dictatorships elsewhere they are often limited only by lack of money and expertise. Tactics can include intimidation, abduction, torture and murder. In Latin America Death Squads kill civilians, journalists, lawyers, trade unionists and leaders of political parties, and go largely unpunished by the security forces – to which, anyway, some belong. In some Western European countries, too, there have been unofficial links between state terror and right-wing terrorists, whose outrages are often indiscriminate. Information is 'passed on', and this 'passing

on' often goes undetected. In times of emergency, some
agencies of state terror secretly counter terrorism against the
state by encouraging unofficial terrorism against suspect targets. For state authorities in general, there are times when it
is convenient for the right hand not to know what the left hand
is doing.

In the West, the constitutional counter-measures of the state
have often been implemented in ways that curtail some civil
liberties without generating mass repression. The main excep-
tion, of course, has been internment in Northern Ireland.
Moreover, weapons technology cuts both ways. The electronic timing-devices of the terrorist are countered by the
robot-sniffers of the state. In Germany and Italy, terrorism led
to a centralisation of counter-terrorist agencies who answered
the ingenuity of selective outrages with sophisticated computer systems and intense forms of surveillance. Terrorism
continues to exert great secret and symbolic power, especially
when it can strike at the heart of its enemy as in the Provisional IRA's Brighton Bombing, the murder of West German
industrialist Hans-Martin Schleyer by the Red Army Faction
(RAF), the Red Brigades' kidnapping of and murder of Italian
political leader Aldo Moro. But state authorities will use the
press and the electronic media to try and obviate the climate of
fear, to orchestrate the outrage as a political spectacle on their
terms, in which publicity is answered by counter-publicity
ten times over, in which suffering and bravery are presented
as the qualities of the victims, brutality and cowardice as the
qualities of the terrorists, firmness and moral principle as the
properties of the state. The authorities and their media gamble
on creating a controlled spectacle to minimise the terrorist's
secret power. It is usually one in which terrorists themselves
are in the wings, the invisible enemies who are never seen and
seldom heard.

In West Germany and Italy the violence culminating in
the outrages of the Red Army Faction and the Red Brigades
changed over time as terror was used as a ritual humiliation
of individual members of the capitalist state.

Theatrical terror which began after 1968 with forms of open
public humiliation by anarchist groups, escalated to wound-
ings and kneecappings of industrialists or public figures by

new terrorist groups, and finally ended in bombings, kidnappings and assassinations. Such outrages demonstrated to the
public and the state that members of the Establishment were
not immune from physical danger. But to succeed they would
still need to rely on mass disaffection. The paradox of terrorism was that it increased its importance as public outrage the
more the utopian culture of mass street protests dissipated.
Its paranoid and dystopian secrecy contrasted unfavourably
with the open spectacle of mass demonstrations, but very
soon it became more newsworthy. It lacked, however, a vital
ingredient, the publicity which could give terror a human face.
Its voices were only heard in the communiqués issued after
outrages, and this gave the state the upper hand as it publicised warnings with mugshots that stigmatised unknown terrorists as common criminals. For many, the first film image of
the reviled terrorist would be at the moment of arrest as, for
example, in the case of the wounded and dishevelled Andreas
Baader. Terrorists may crave publicity in a media age but
governments under attack usually try to ensure they never
get the kind of publicity they want, that instead they have
no one to speak for them. By the time the terrorist faces trial,
his or her image has been dehumanised. In the Red Brigade,
trial defendants were put behind cages for 'security' reasons
but the sight on television of the accused terrorists gave them
the appearance of caged animals, putting them on a par at
best with football hooligans and at worst, with murderous
psychopaths.

Interestingly, with the trial of the Baader–Meinhof group
in May 1975 terrorist paratheatre in West Germany changed
back to absurdist theatre, and social drama became courtroom
melodrama. But this was modernist melodrama, a fractured
Theatre of the Absurd rather than a Hollywood spectacular.[3]
During the two-year trial the defendants constantly insulted
not only the presiding federal judges but also their defending
lawyers. All members of the judiciary, whether sympathetic
or hostile, were denounced as 'arseholes' and the courtroom
drama consisted of disruptive devices used by the four terrorists to ignore questions and change the scenario of the
debate by attempting to accuse their accusers of crimes against
humanity. The court responded to their sustained venom by

switching off and removing their microphones. The defendants responded by leaving the courtroom. The trial continued with or without their presence.

These tactics were opportunistic but also borne out of desperation. And they were self-defeating. When any statement
made by lawyers was either ignored or drowned out by
staged tantrums, their supporters in the courtroom relished
the drama. But in refusing to accept any rational discourse
about the justice of their treatment, the group dismally failed
to communicate their grievances to a wider public. They
were instead committed to the continuation of terror by other
means. Indeed, long before the end they had become impo-
tent terrorists vainly trying to practise their profession while
incarcerated in cells adjacent to the courtroom. Their daily life
consisted of the movement between courtroom melodrama
and a naturalist prison which was anything but natural. Inside
Stammheim the increased level of regimentation, the surveillance through the bugging of cells and the accumulative stress
of physical isolation, were facts lost to the trial by the fren-
zied contempt of the defendants. Effective in disrupting the
practices of the court, and driving at least one judge to the
point of nervous breakdown, they were powerless to alter the
increasing oppressiveness of their prison lives.[4]

The isolation of the 'terrorist cell' in the world at large has
its ironic mirror-image in the isolation of the terrorist cell in
jail. The seventh floor at Stammheim was set aside for Baader,
Raspe, Ennslin and Meinhof, the two women separated from
the two men by cells, the men and women separated from
each other by partitions through which they could talk but
do little else. The theatre enters too into their growing isolation and the paranoia it projects. Their favourite play was
Brecht's *Die Massnahme (The Measures Taken)*, which deals
with revolutionary fratricide and finally justifies it. Brecht's
four Russian agitators on their Chinese mission are forced
to kill their fifth Young Comrade whose conscience and pity
foil, they claim, their objective revolutionary aims. Infecting
the Baader–Meinhof group was a collective paranoia about
defectors, of whom there were several turning State's evidence, and it came to a head with their growing hostility toward
Ulrike Meinhof who committed suicide before the end of the

trial. The group had no official leader but, following the work of fiction they most admired, *Moby Dick*, they gave members Red Army Faction code names based on the novel's characters. Predictably, Baader, who spent much of his spare time reading Mickey Mouse books, was Captain Ahab.[5] The champions of the isolated 'terrorist cell' found themselves in a different kind of cell with a different kind of isolation where they retained their sense of theatricality but lost their perspective on the world.

In *Die Massnahme* Brecht tried to add a new tragic dimension to his epic theatre, the Party as Destiny, replacing the gods and the natural order that prevailed in previous tragic forms. It was a bold and perverse concept. But for the Red Army Faction there was not even a Party as Destiny. They had no real constituency. Their fate thus moves from tragedy into the realm of melodrama or, at best, grotesque farce. The idea that social drama can in fact mimic dramatic forms, a version of life imitating art, appears also in Erica Wagner-Pacifici's illuminating study of the 1978 kidnapping of Aldo Moro,[6] an event itself given spectacular form in the Yugoslav street-theatre production of L. Ristić. Wagner-Pacifici's concern is to show how an incident of great political complexity comes to be simplified in its 'theatrical' re-presentation by the protagonists themselves, by media reportage, and by public response. Thus a complex historical event which ends in tragic loss and shows good and evil on both sides is simplified into a black-and-white picture of the world.[7] The choice is between the Establishment and the terrorists and, for either side, failure to make a choice is seen as backsliding or treachery.

In the drama which followed the kidnapping, Aldo Moro became 'Aldo Moro', not a tough Christian Democrat who came to respect his kidnappers and to plead with the author-ities to ensure his release, but a noble martyr who represented all of Italy. a symbol of all that was great in the nation, held against his will and defiant to the end. At one point during his captivity there was a 'Moro is not Moro' movement which included a petition by fifty close friends and associates claiming that the Moro who wrote from the People's prison was not the Moro they had known. The clear implication was that they did not want to know the 'Moro' in captivity. The Christian Democrats, the centrist parties, the Communists

and the mass media for once were united in their view that the
attack on Moro was really an attack on the democratic system.
Thus the theatre of communiqués, by which the Red Brigades
sought to show their symbolic power, backfired. From their
unseen hideout, they were presented as masked or invisible
monsters. State propaganda invoked the terror of the mask
concealing the unknown.

Wagner-Pacifici notes that the age of modernity which produces sophisticated terror also produces dramatic self-consciousness. Through newspapers, magazines, radio, television, video and film we are now saturated with communications which set up expectations about the dramaturgy
of 'events'. They are meant to have a beginning, a middle
and an end, a complicated plot with ingenious twists, a
serial narrative fed to us in simplified form.[8] We live in an
increasingly dramatised society in which we are increasingly
aware of the importance of performance – our own as well as
that of others. But the attempts of the Red Brigades to mimic
the courts of the authorities and set up their own 'people's
courts' in anonymous cellars was a masquerade which failed,
a theatre in a remote cave to which no one came. It was further
proof that those who possess the means of communication
ultimately decide what is or is not spectacle. By uniting the
media and the political parties against them, the Red Brigades,
in the subsequent transfer of phony theatre into public melodrama, quite easily became the faceless villains. The killing
of Moro was seen by almost no one as justice carried out by
a court acting in the name of the people. On the contrary, it
was seen by nearly everyone as murder most foul carried out
by melodramatic villains.

II

The theatre of terror as it has developed in this century is in no
sense a unified form, nor is terror a separate theme easily isolated. We find it in German Expressionism, in Brechtian epic
tragedy, in the ludic theatre of Beckett and Pinter, the liturgic
and ritual extravagances of Genet and Soyinka, the melodrama of Sam Shepard, John Guare amd Trevor Griffiths, in the
new 'Jacobean' political theatre of Edward Bond, Howard
Brenton, David Hare and Howard Barker in the seventies,

and in the grotesque farce of Max Frisch and Dario Fo. Brecht's
Die Massnahme is a more violent play than many others in
the epic tradition. To the Brechtian tradition of the V-effect
(from *Verfremdungseffekt*) which forces the spectator to judgement through the unexpected altering of circumstance, Bond
adds the 'Aggro-effects' of *Lear* which force commitment
on the spectator through unexpected forms of violence. The
most successful among these forms, it seems to me, are
those which dramatise terror by distancing us from it, while
re-staging its menace and its climate of fear. Those plays which
merely play upon the propinquity or topicality of terror, or
present its moral relativities purely as a political issue, are
often the least compelling. What is often taken as the most
pressing issue of the day in media melodrama works best in
theatre when it is devoid of melodramatic content. This is not
to say that the theatre should ignore terror as spectacle – it
always needs to embody it in some form – but that it should
find jarring ways of estranging us from it in an age of dramatic
self-consciousness where performance is often regarded as an
aggressive thrusting of spectacle in the faces of its spectators.

The point is a difficult one to make, for it is the immediacy
of terror, its literal and metaphorical explosiveness, which
has inspired dramatists the world over. The renaissance of a
political theatre in Europe, and particularly in Britain, owes
much to the engagement with wider moral issues raised
by terrorism. The advent of terror has repoliticised theatre
in a very important and necessary way. But only up to a
point. Immediacy is best answered by the power of ultimate
detachment, a detachment embedded in stagecraft and form.
For that reason I wish to argue that the following plays are
among the most important in the dramatisation of terror in
the last thirty years: Pinter's *The Dumb Waiter* (1959), Genet's
The Blacks (1967), Bond's *Lear* (1970), Hampton's *Savages* (1974).
Fo's *Accidental Death of an Anarchist* (1974), Beckett's *Catastrophe*
(1982), Brenton's *The Churchill Play* (1974) and the *The Romans
in Britain* (1980), Soyinka's *A Play of Giants* (1984) and Arthur
Kopit's *End of the World* (1984). The following are among the
important plays I feel have failed to find an effective form:
Shepard's *Operation Sidewinder* (1969), Brenton's *Weapons of
Happiness* (1976) and *Magnificence* (1973), Bond's *The Worlds*

(1980), Griffith's *Real Dreams* (1987), Howard Barker's *That Good Between Us* (1977) and *Credentials of a Sympathiser* (1979). Ron Hutchinson's *Rat in the Skull* (1984), and Pinter's *One for the Road* (1984). The lists are provocative. Some playwrights appear on both. For that reason the question has to be asked. Is the division critical whimsy or does it have a genuine rationale in the nature and development of dramatic form?

Predictably, I would suggest the latter. The major dramas of terrorism are works in which displacement in space and time, dystopia and play, are all eminent features. The epic tragedy of Bond, the tragic farce of Fo, and the 'complete art-work' of Beckett or Heiner Müller come immediately to mind. Here the plays concerned find new forms of tragedy or farce as effective dramatic weapons. In the case of the plays which fail through didactic immediacy, the dramaturgy treads an uneasy path between realism and melodrama. despite the clear influence of Brecht. At the same time, space-time displacement and forms of play and dystopia are much less evident. The failure of a generic drama of the terrorist present arises from the fact that the theatre follows too closely, though not consciously, the sensibility of media saturation when its politics are diametrically opposed to it; opposed, that is, to the media's complicity in controlled anti-terrorist spectacle. The drama thus takes on a cultural form similar to that of its ideological enemies. It lacks estranging devices from that burning presentness which is distinctive of most media coverage of terrorism. Here, in press, radio and television, what Adorno calls the cult of information is used as a vehicle for serial melodrama. The drama of terror by contrast, I want to argue, works best when it stands back, when it distances the spectator through play or farce as in Dario Fo's *Accidental Death of an Anarchist*, or when it distances its tragic action through gestic extremes of space and time. In this respect, I would like to compare Pinter, Bond and Brenton with one another, to contrast displacement and presentness in their work, and to look more closely at the theatricality of terror and at why the theatre does not become merely an adjunct to normal conventions of terror as spectacle.

One of the vital ingredients here may be humour. Pinter's *The Dumb Waiter* is a classic but also prophetic tragicomedy because it shows terrorists without a cause, victims of their necessary secrecy, and of the devaluation of value which dogs their footsteps. Their leader is unseen, the victim for whom they wait not yet known. Hilariously, Gus and Joe try to piece together where they are by speculating on whether the football teams they have watched are playing at home or away. Thrust together in a basement room they share the claustrophobic anticipation of the violent act to come with a growing unease. The room separates them from a world of public knowledge outside. Though the pervasive menace of play, the terrorists become terrorised by the 'dumb waiter', the neutral medium of terror which feeds them with more and more outrageous menus that they strive in vain to satisfy. In the basement room the assassins are themselves terrorised by the unknown 'outside' or 'above', the insidious game they presume their unseen boss is playing with them. Only in the very last scene do we see that the victim is to be one of the assassins, for whom the other waits, not knowing his identity until he bursts into the room. It remains a marvellous dramatic coup. The rebellious assassin is about to be killed by his partner who has obeyed orders to the last. The self-inflicted wounds of terror which have been notorious from Nechayev until the terror groups of the seventies, the Japanese Red Army, the Baader–Meinhof group and the Weather Underground are shown here with great dramatic power in what is a highly ludic theatre.

Pinter refuses to name names, context, circumstance or motive. Terror and resistance come through the menace of play. The dumb waiter is a superb metonym of unanticipated terror, as comic as it is macabre. The element of play is both comic and serious: at one point Gus asks of his unseen boss, 'What's his game?' The formalism is exonerated by the effectiveness of play within the form. In the interrogation in *One for the Road*, however, it seems to me that Pinter's formalism runs into difficulties. The form is naturalistic, the interrogation of the victims unrelenting, the victims themselves mute, unresisting. Pinter wants to take us to that harrowing moment when resistance has been broken by the agents of state terror, when there is no longer any come-back and where the victims are not themselves a terrorist cell, but a respectable bourgeois family with offending political opinions. There is no doubt that Pinter's play is powerful and gruelling – actors themselves find

it harrowing to act. But its one-dimensional focus is not only
too oppressive but also too veiled. We do not know who,
why, where or how – questions the naturalistic form invites
us to ask. We do not witness a theatricality which permits us
to stand back and judge. We do not have the political context
of arrest, or the outcome of torture. We have instead Pinter's
attempt to evoke through the chilling gesture and the chilling
phrase the ubiquitous state terror of the modern world. But
here his obliqueness ends in obfuscation.

Nonetheless, the advantage of Pinter's method can seen in
comparison with Ron Hutchinson's *Rat in the Skull* which more
clearly states a context. An RUC officer arrives in England to
interrogate a suspected IRA prisoner and proceeds to evade
the judicial constraints on interrogation. The interrogation
in which the prisoner does resist is powerful at times but
sometimes lapses into the posturing clichés of melodrama, a
trap against which Pinter's ludic formalism protects him. But
the one-dimensional theatricality of both plays can be seen
in comparison with two others that do show, in contrasting
ways, the theatricality of interrogation. In Beckett's *Catastrophe*, even more formal and minimalist than Pinter's *One for
the Road*, the muteness of the victim is taken to its logical
conclusion. The piece, which is about a rehearsal in which
the protagonist is reduced to an object by a director and his
female assistant who put him on a plinth and treat him like a
tailor's dummy, uses theatricality itself as a metaphor for degradation. It is dedicated to Vaclav Havel. On a different plane,
Christopher Hampton's *Savages* shows terror with resistance
and without it. Its dramatic impact derives from the stark
juxtaposition of the two in the state-sponsored terror against
Brazilian Indians and the kidnapping of a British diplomat by
urban guerillas. The counterpoint of the dual terror working in
opposite directions fits with the epic style of intercutting short
precise scenes and flashbacks, but also fits the play's paradox.
The common educated background of West, the aptly named
diplomat, and Carlos, his kidnapper, gives their abrasive dialogue a witty and acerbic flavour. The Indians are 'savages',
however, beyond the pale and beyond discourse. There is no
dialogue before death as there is in the case of the murdered
West, only genocide on a mass scale. The dialogic relationship

of the two intellectuals, Carlos and West, kidnapper and kidnapped, contrasts with the mute terror of the rapacious state
and its unheard victims.

Hampton's play works because it takes its English hero
out of the parochial world of British politics and places him
in a global context. The kidnapping of diplomats has been a
common feature of seventies terrorism but Hampton finds a
deeper dimension by showing the double powerlessness of his
English diplomat. Powerless to do anything about the Indians
he wishes to protect, he is also powerless to prevent his own
murder at the hands of guerillas, and unable to obtain the
release of the political prisoners for whom he is a bargaining
chip. West is both naive and sceptical; his captor is committed but finally not ruthless or clever enough to be triumphant.
The dialogue between them is electrifying, a quality largely
missing from the English political theatre of the same decade.
I say this specifically with reference to contemporary Britain
where I find it a curious deficiency in the plays about the ultra-
left by Barker, Brenton, Bond and Hare. All are didacticians,
never ceasing to tell us about the ideological principles of their
Marxist dramaturgy. But they are curiously unable to invest
their characters with the power of the idea – any idea. The
young Trotskyist workers in *Weapons of Happiness*, the squatters in *Magnificence*, the clowning duet of *That Good between Us*,
the cartoon negotiators in *Credentials of a Sympathiser*, the inept
kidnappers in *The Worlds*, the hippie-rapping self-dramatising
revolutionaries of *Real Dreams*, are all diminished and depleted
figures who might work well in tragicomedy or farce because
of the grandiose absurdity of their aspirations. Unfortunately,
most of them are too stupid to be taken seriously as figures in
a moral discourse. Yet that is how they are viewed by their
respective dramatists, and that is how prospective audiences
are required to see them.

In a way this is rough justice. Griffiths, Bond, Brenton and
Barker have spent considerable effort on revolutionary manifestos and statements. But little of their powers of abstrac-
tion, little of the energy that goes into such statements, have
appeared in the dramatic speeches of their recent characters.
Here the dominant form is a truncated and illiterate spilling-
out of half-sentences without main clause or transitive verb, a

shorthand of the mind which results in a nervy fast-food conception of ideology as disposable junk. Language is compelled
to be blunt and plain, creating a macho directness which is
usually a union of dramatic convenience and radical style. Fair
enough. Brenton's early dramaturgy has its political origins
in the French Situationism of 1968. But it translates uneasily
into British circumstance. Instead of a powerful ideological
rejection of established ideologies, we have a strange
diffidence to ideology as if it can only be dramatised by being
dismembered and strewn around in meaningless fragments.
Anyone trying to string together anything which smacks of
eloquence is 'slagged off', to use an English idiom, by his
fellow-revolutionaries. And yet the ideological language is
still used *ad nauseam*. This is not to say that class-enemies come
off any better. They invariably come off worse, but this is
largely because they lack the chumminess of the brittle
revolutionaries. Moreover, the structures of feeling in these
works are usually, to go back to Joyce, ones of extreme
loathing – loathing by terrorists of their victims, loathing by
well-heeled victims of the terrorists, and excessive
self-loathing by the hero-terrorists which means they do not
have a good word to say about themselves. To top it all, there
is a sporadic loathing of all the characters by their
neo-Jacobean authors.

One riposte would be to stress the core of the method used
by Brenton and others, that is, the self-contained scene which
is both powerful and explosive and which demands that the
audience work it through. Brenton argues that his characters
move quickly and explosively from innocence to experience
and have time to dwell on the past. Each scene is a flash-fire
quickly over. This method often works with great results but
it also diminishes perspective and the accretive effect of gestic
images. It lacks what Bond himself claims has always been
important: a unified style. The past and the future, play
and farce, demand a more deeply-rooted structure. Two of
the great epic tragedies of recent English writing are Bond's
Lear and Brenton's *The Romans in Britain*. Both, however, are
dystopian dramas, self-consciously aware of the ascendancy
of terror in the betrayal of ideals. In that respect they are
plays that mark the beginning and the end of the decade.
Bond's epic recreation of Shakespeare enables him to see the

symbiotic relationship between state terror and revolutionary terrorism. Brenton's dual staging of the Romans in Britain (against the Celts) and the British in Ireland (also against the Celts) ironises the mythology of imperialism but also focuses on that same symbiotic relationship. The dystopian terror of recent times is stronger here when dramatised in the past than it is in the up-to-date trashing of class-enemies and fellow-travellers in *Magnificence* or the more impressive *Weapons of Happiness*.

There are several ironies in the complex relationship between the spectacularity of terrorism and the theatricality of terror. Both seem to be bred out of a consumer culture of immediacy, of which terrorism is a grotesque mirror-image, and out of a dystopian concern, bordering on despair, with the immediacy of spectacular action. Terrorism combines in its macabre way the logic of performance with the logic of despair. It is the public staging of grotesque and murderous farce which, at its most effective, is transformed into a collective nightmare. That is why in some political dramas the didactic acclaiming of terrorist heroes seems morally threadbare, and yet it is a trap into which at times many playwrights fall. The disgust with amorality and corruption in the political order is one of the most potent features in the contemporary drama of terrorism. But it must be tempered by a refusal to be entranced by violent response. Where it is, then the drama of terror as a public cultural form has much to offer us.

Finally, one might want to note the also exemplary form of dealing with state terror used by Wole Soyinka in his recent tragicomedy *A Play of Giants*. Set in the Bugaran embassy overlooking the United Nations in New York, it is the story of the last days of Field-Marshall Kamini, facing a popular uprising back home in a Bugara racked by financial ruin and despotic terror. A sculptor is making a life-size effigy of Kamini while a doting Scandinavian journalist, various acolytes and African despots play up to the self-styled genius. Soyinka's play owes much to *The Balcony*, which he acknowledges, in its play on the hollow idols of power confronted by revolution. But Kamini never allows himself to be impersonated. Instead, he acts out his own masquerade as master of the universe while all is falling around him. As he goes through the motions of omnipotence, he casually uses the toilet backstage as a torture chamber for those who have offended him. The chairman of the Bugaran bank who had inadvertently let slip the fact that Bugaran currency is as worthless as toilet paper ends up in the toilet being tortured by a Task Force Special as Kamini holds court outside. The foregrounding of power against a background of terror is enhanced by the later torturing of the sculptor who has indiscreetly let slip to Kamini's journalist his opinion that the sculpture should be in Madame Tussaud's Chamber of Horrors and not facing the United Nations. The two, power and terror, come together when the sculptor, swathed in bandages from head to foot, is led back to work past an astonished UN Secretary-General. Predictably, Kamini acts as if nothing has happened.

The use of dramatic space is reinforced here by the use of language. That of Kamini's acolytes is the formal and hypocritical language of political deference while Kamini's pidgin English with its absurd semantic aspirations to greatness is a language of gutter fascism. It is a language behind the official language of politics in the same way that the terror backstage is the action 'behind' the official audiences that Kamini grants to his visiting dignitaries. At one stage. Soyinka drives home the comic point by having two Soviet diplomats insult Kamini in Russian while delivering effusive homilies to him in English. The mixture of buffoonery and terror brings Genet's house of illusions neatly back into the material arena of the contemporary political stage, where, however, political reality appears as completely surreal. In a final absurd *Götterdämerung*, demonstrators gather outside the embassy in protest against Kamini, while he takes all his visiting diplomats hostage and turns his grenade-launchers against the United Nations building opposite. The farce of self-destruction ends in a pandemonium of frightening unrest. At the moment of his nemesis, Soyinka's most compelling villain has become the ultimate global terrorist.

NOTES

1. *The Critical Writings of James Joyce* (New York: The Viking Press, 1959), 143-4.
2. See Richard E. Rubenstein, *Alchemists of Revolution: Terrorism in the Modern World* (London: Taurus Books, 1987), 54ff. Rubenstein defines terrorism as 'acts of small-group violence for which arguable claims of mass representation can be made.' Ibid., 31.
3. The definitive account of the Stammheim trial is given by Stefan Aust, *The Baader–Meinhhof Group*, trans. Anthea Bell (London: The Bodley Head, 1987), 295ff. The courtroom was built from prefabricated parts in a potato field adjacent to the prison.
4. Ibid., 425ff.
5. Ibid., 427ff.
6. Robin Erica Wagner-Pacifici, *The Moro Morality Play: Terrorism as Social Drama* (Chicago: University of Chicago Press, 1986).
7. Ibid., 7ff.
8. Ibid., 231ff.

3

The Inverted World of Spectacle:
Social and Political Responses to Terrorism

AIDA HOZIC

The morning of 26 April 1988 might have been like any other mellow spring morning in Italy had it not been for a rather unusual terrorist attack. An anonymous pro-Palestinian terrorist organisation, advocating a boycott of Israeli products, injected a blue 'poisonous' substance into seventy-five 'Jaffa' grapefruit on sale in Italy. Although the terrorists immediately proclaimed that their action was purely symbolic – since the insides of the poisoned grapefruit were dyed blue, they were easily recognisable and thus avoidable – the state and social response far exceeded the potential threat. The Ministry of Health ordered a seizure of all grapefruit on Italian territory and had policemen run from one shop to another in order to collect the fruit. Shipments were stopped not only from the Near East but from other regions of the world as well. Israel immediately joined the grapefruit hunters by sending its secret agents to Italy. The best Italian research institutes, though baffled by the nature of the alleged poison, firmly stated that it was toxic. Consequently, patients with symptoms of 'terrible poisoning' appeared in hospitals and the media linked the survival of the Italian nation to the survival of several grapefruit-fed guinea pigs. When the toxicologists finally recognised their mistake, and reluctantly confessed that the mysterious substance was just a non-toxic colouring regularly used in pharmacies and kitchens, 360 tons of grapefruit were brought back to the shops. Yet their consumption continued to decrease even in the following months, as the images of fruit dumped into the sea and the squealing of guinea pigs remained deeply imprinted in the collective memory.

As so often in the past, the terrorists eventually succeeded in their aim, thanks to the disproportionate state and social response. As so often in the past, the immanent spectacularity of terrorism was used as an excuse for the attention devoted to the 'terrorist threat'. There was nothing inherently spectacular about the yellow grapefruit with blue interiors sitting on supermarket shelves. Nevertheless, the action was called 'dramatic', 'spectacular', and even, as Israeli officials put it, 'a clamorous act of sabotage against the heart of Israel'.[1]

This essay, which focuses on the social and political responses to terrorism, will: a) re-examine this notion of the intrinsic spectacularity of terrorism, too often used as justification for the extreme efficiency of contemporary terrorism to be taken for granted; b) show that terrorism is initially a paratheatrical phenomenon which the state and society 'spectacularise' in order to satisfy some of their particular needs; c) analyse the benefits and costs of this 'spectacularisation'.

Spectacularity vs Theatricality

In the last twenty years, it has been stated many times that one of the main characteristics of modern terrorism is its ability to attract public attention.[2] In a world which has already reached its saturation point as far as information is concerned, only violence, it was argued, could break through the wall of global indifference. This 'visibility' of violence was the main reason why minor and marginalised groups, whose aim was presumably mere self-propaganda, would resort to terrorism. Unlike any other political activity, terrorism could give these groups immediate recognition on a world-wide scale. At the same time, this visibility was primarily attributed to the expansion of the media and its tendency to overdramatise events. Thus, it seemed logical to conclude that terrorism was efficient due to its presence in the media and, as a corollary to this, that there would be no terrorism if there were no television.[3] The main problem with this argument was not that it was unconvincing – on the contrary, it found its implementation in various forms of media censorship in several countries – but that it was oversimplified and fundamentally wrong.

It has rarely been taken into account that terrorism is not a static, but a dynamic phenomenon. There were certain periods, early on, when terrorists were absolutely unable to attract public attention – if that was their goal at all. There were cases not only of unreported mass violence but also of certain types of terrorism which never made their way to the front pages.[4] Moreover, it is in the nature of the media to select and present the news according to the perceived desires of their public; the media reflect both the prevailing power structure and the deep, and perhaps unconscious, wishes of society. In other words, it has rarely been considered that the 'spectacularity' of terrorism might have been a product not only of the symbolic nature of terrorist activities, but also of certain social and political needs. Such spectacularity would then be a value added, so to speak, to certain events, and not an inherent characteristic of them.

In the late sixties, Guy Debord, leader of the Situationist movement, warned against the new emerging dictator: the spectacular state. 'Spectacularity', wrote Debord, 'is not just a mere set of images, but a set of human relationships mediated by images. . . . All of that which was once an immediate experience transformed itself [in a spectacle] into a representation.'[5]

The concepts 'theatrical' and 'spectacular' will be used in this paper in Debord's sense – not as 'higher' or 'lesser' visual or aesthetic forms but as sociopolitical categories. According to Italian theatre historian Luigi Allegri, theatre and spectacle have completely different origins, different relationships with audiences and actors, and even different inherent conceptions of time and space.[6] Consequently, their social functions are very distinct.

Spectacle, according to Allegri, operates as a politically institutionalised form. From the Greek Odeon, which had an educational function, through the Roman *panem et circenses*, to our contemporary sport events, spectacle has always been the exclusive patrimony of the official power. Power adores spectacle – it is always represented at spectacles there by shiny uniforms, distant but appealing speakers, red carpets and routine actions – since spectacle allows official power to present itself as a divine, untouchable and often depersonalised *perpetuum mobile*. The actors and the audience in the spectacle are physically separated, and participation is replaced by the observation of breathtaking events which can be admired or feared. The spectacular action generally complies with the secret desires of the audience; it is that which the public is willing to see and it induces ecstasy, not catharsis, among those who attend it.

Theatre, on the other hand, derives from popular ritual, and preserves an ambivalent relationship with the established order. The world of theatre is rarely a 'pleasuredome', since it often enacts the truths which we would rather forget. Theatrical action compels the audience to re-examine its own deeply ingrained world views by confronting it with a sort of existential play on the stage. This active participation goes even a step further in festivals and carnivals, the best-known forms of diffuse theatricality. In such forms, the formal division of actor from audience disappears, as well as the given pretext of the drama. In their spontaneous recreation of the microcosm, festivals rely on the 'common' world and 'common' people, not on professionals. The streets are transformed into stages, and servants into kings, so the public not only contemplates but virtually enacts a different social order.

In the Middle Ages, the festivals were a sort of controlled or channeled dissent, an inversion of power in a medieval community, an attempt to turn the world upside-down.[7] In modern times, institutionalised and reduced to a mere holiday, they lost their importance. But theatrical elements are preserved in populist movements, revolutions and upheavals.[8] Diffuse theatricality and insurrections have in common some very important elements – the tendency to include as many actors as possible, to annul real time and establish a new one, to display by immediate example that the recreation of the world is feasible. Moreover, theatricality and insurrections both display violence. Regardless of their jovial character, festivals themselves have never been a peaceful manifestation of inverted power, but rather a disturbing admixture of the celebration and the destruction of life. The difference is that what was once a mere grotesque has now become a real, macabre performance.

Therefore, theatricality and spectacularity are similar to the extent that both can be used as *forms of expression* for symbolic political power, as indispensable elements of any political activity in search of popular support. However, they obviously diverge in the ways by which this support is acquired, as well as in the kind of support they manage to elicit.

Spectacle increases the gap between the actor and audience, between the empowered and the powerless. But, as a form which pleases the audience, it also reduces conflict and social tension. Theatrical action, on the other hand, questions everything, reopens hidden conflicts and taboos, and attempts to mobilise, not satisfy, the audience.

Applying these concepts to terrorism is not an easy task. Terrorism is a complex communicational mechanism. It has diverse messages for various segments of society. There are those whom it wants to threaten and those whom it means to attract. The 'marketing' of actions varies from one group to the other. Yet, assuming that terrorism starts with an aim to recruit new followers by exposing society to a simulated 'crisis situation' – or, as Rapoport says, by 'generat[ing] mass insurrection by means of provocation'[9] – then it should obviously be regarded as a paratheatrical form. This theatricality can also be considered as one of the major sources of terrorist threat. Terrorism frightens not only because some people are and others may become victims of the crisis, but also because some other people could find the idea of 'simulation' attractive. The fear that terrorism may outgrow its own limits and transform itself into a general dissent is probably the crucial reason why its 'theatricality' had to be combated and transformed into global 'spectacle'.

The Benefits of Spectacularisation

One of the main assumptions of this essay is that both state and society derive benefit from the spectacularisation of terrorism, since, otherwise, their disproportionate response to terrorism would not make much sense. It may seem absurd that it is possible to benefit from action directed against oneself by simply manipulating its form; however, 'The Grapefruit Affair' may be used as a paradigm for tangible gains from spectacularisation. Grapefruit 'poisoning' was the last and evidently the least dangerous of the events which disturbed Italian public opinion during the month of April 1988. On the 13th, a bomb presumably set by a radical-left group destroyed the bookshop of a homosexual, Jewish leader of the Green party in Turin. On the 14th, in front of a bar which was a regular meeting-place for American marines and officers in Naples, another bomb killed five people and wounded dozens of others. On the 16th, the Red Brigades killed Roberto Ruffilli, Senator of the Christian Democrat Party. On the same day, Abu Jihad, a leader of the PLO, was killed in his house in Tunisia, allegedly by the Mossad. On the 19th, the Italian Ministry of the Interior received the first anonymous calls regarding the grapefruit, but did nothing until the first 'poisonous' sample was found.

Italian police and the new government, inaugurated only a day before the Naples bombing, managed to identify some of the presumed terrorists, but none were arrested. Yet the new government did manage to endanger its already problematic relationship with Israel by directly accusing it at a UN meeting of Abu Jihad's assassination.

Therefore, the 'Grapefruit Affair' was in many respects a blessing for the Italian state machinery. By simply seizing everything that could have been seized – obviously a much easier task than finding terrorists – the government managed to show that it could still protect its citizens from the terrorist threat. Also, since the grapefruit 'poisoning' gained much more publicity than any of the preceding terrorist actions, people finally got a chance to express all their accumulated fear and enjoy the pleasure of common concern. Finally, the cooperation between Italian and Israeli officials in grapefruit hunting was an excellent opportunity for the two countries to make 'peace' in a diplomatic way. Thus, the mechanisms employed in the spectacularisation of the 'Grapefruit Affair', and the benefits from it were relatively easy to detect. However, in the case of West–European left-wing terrorism, on which we shall now focus, those mechanisms were usually much more subtle and lacking in immediate gains.

Left-wing terrorism had a completely different treatment in the West-European media than did Middle-Eastern, national-secessionist or even right-wing terrorism. With the benefit of hindsight, it also becomes evident that different countries, specifically Italy, Germany and France, dealt with their own left-wing terrorism in diverse ways. So far, the explanations

of this differentiated approach have been purely political, ascribing the manipulation of terrorism to the government's 'leftist' or 'rightist' preferences. The sphere of social response, except for vague 'mentality' arguments, has been largely neglected.

Several years ago, Phil Cerny rightly argued that the political significance of modern terrorism 'lies less in its organisational or violent manifestations than in its interactions with the social formation and political system in which it occurs.'[10] Hence, the symbolic power of terrorism should be analysed in the context of the prevailing political and social circumstances in the countries concerned. Left-wing terrorism was presumably a rebellion of European middle-class youth against the complacent liberal optimism of their parents. If so, the hypothesis may be put forward that the 'existential dread'[11] stemming from the left-wing terrorism was a far greater threat than that coming from 'aliens', be they Arabs or Bretons, or historically proven 'vandals' such as fascists. This is so for three reasons. First, it could have meant having a revolution in one's own backyard. Second, the tendency to exclude 'violence' from the civilised, rational, democratic Western world and label all those who practice it as 'barbarians' goes as far back as ancient Greece.[12] Third, it was not directed against any actual political order but against an *ideal* political order.

In order to explain left-wing terrorism, to justify the fight against it and at the same time preserve the myth of Western civilisation as a Garden of Eden, European left-wing terrorists had first to be presented as 'deviants', 'criminals', foreign agents' – as strangers in their own societies. Their actions were to be viewed as a 'catastrophe', a non-human, irrational evil. On the political level, exaggeration of the threat could have been intended to reinforce or even create public political consensus in Western Europe.

Spectacularisation as an Enclosure of the Image

West European left-wing terrorism, as substantial empirical evidence suggests, stems from the 1968 student movement.[13] While the debates still continue as to whether the movement was one of the last moments of the eighteenth century or the advent of the twenty-first, as the fact remains that 1968 was one of the greatest recreations of Medieval festivity in the last few centuries. The student movement was a challenge not only to the established political order but to the very foundation of modern western civilisation: its rationality based on scientific empiricism, economic efficiency and political liberalism. The idea of the theatre was also changing at the time. Streets became theatrical while the politicised 'living' theatre moved down to the streets. The protests often had their own choreographies, staging and costumes. Theatre paraphernalia ranged from the coffins used in demonstration Against the Atom Death in the FRG to the 'flower-power' symbols indispensable to every anti-Vietnam War protest. The element of play persisted for a long time and the fine line between the burning of paper effigies of political figures and attacks on real people was not crossed for several years. Yet, the mass-society authorities symbolised or embodied in impersonal buildings, flags and police were not only laughed at but also violently attacked. Manuals describing how to make the Bomb were just as much mandatory reading as the writings of Mao and Lenin. Thriving on this violent culture, which found its justification in the writings of such intellectuals as Sartre[14] and Marcuse,[15] terrorism in its early days developed as a radicalisation of the 'fiesta'. It was a play set in motion over which its authors had lost control. Once the movement was over, the first terrorist organisations, formed as a consequence. Their principal aim was precisely to reinforce the festival atmosphere, to continue to recreate the days of 1968 with their revolutionary enthusiasm, primordial social order and extraordinary feeling of solidarity and belonging. In the early eighties, Renato Curcio, leader of the historical nucleus of the Italian Red Brigades (Brigate Rosse), still wrote (inspired by the works of Mikhail Bakhtin) that 'cultural revolution in metropolis is the construction of festivity – as a vision of the world oriented towards the future'.[16]

The dynamics of terrorism is still relatively unexplored terrain,[17] but it seems that all the terrorist organisations formed in Western Europe after the dissolution of the 1968 movement went through roughly three stages. They started with acts of common violence and provocation, moved on to naive kidnapping and symbolic violence, and only at the end resorted to attacks on people and premeditated assassination.

Initially, terrorism represented a paratheatrical phenomenon, and the actions of organised clandestine groups were hardly distinguishable from those undertaken by the majority of the movement. In addition to being openly violent, both were still characterised by elements of play and 'inversions' of power; by close, often personal relationships with both potential sympathisers and enemies (e.g., the Red Brigades installed themselves in factories and searched for their victims among managerial staff and for supporters among the workers); and by an important moral component which made terrorists look more like Robin Hoods of modern time than bloodthirsty pirates. The first registered 'terrorist' action in West Berlin was a famous 'pudding case' which took place in 1967. Kommune 1, obsessed with 'deeds not words' propaganda, prepared a 'welcome cake' for American Vice-President Hubert Humphrey. The cake, as in slapstick American comedies, was supposed to be thrown in his face, but the police prevented it. Newspapers reported that the pudding was indeed a bomb. Bommi Bauman, leader of the 2 June terrorist group, formed on the ashes of Kommune 1, writes in his autobiography[18] that even though involved in arson and bombings, he and his comrades most enjoyed making false-alarm phone calls to the police. They would announce the presence of a bomb somewhere and then watch from a bar on the other side of the street how the police did the job for them, demolishing the whole building in order to find the bomb. Those who still remember the early days of terrorism would probably recall that for every actual bomb there were at least two which had never ever been found. 'Public trials', the most popular form of terrorist action in Italy, were initially held in factories, and rarely reported by the official press. The 'sentences' and 'executions' came only later on. For a few years, the 'trials' remained the 'theatre', in much the same way as gallows were built as 'inversions' of the spectacle of public torture during festival days. As late as 1975, capital punishment could still consist of shaving a victim's head and tying him to a tree as happened to a Fiat manager. In the same Fiat plant, in 1973, another manager was forced to crawl around the factory on his knees as a false king – a pot on his head instead of crown – while the workers replaced him in the office.

When the process of 'spectacularisation' starts, violence may be benign or deadly, but the terrorist threat to the social order is definitively perceived. The media's main goal becomes not only to confirm the threat, but also to suppress the implicit offer of a different social order, contained in the terrorist 'counter-community'[19] full of illegal 'moralistic' judges, social 'protectors' and 'benefactors'. The image of the terrorists is changed. They are deprived of their human faces and presented as angry monsters – Meinhof's photograph at the moment of arrest is the best example of this.[20] Networks of personal contacts are substituted by an image on TV where terrorism seems as distant and devoid of reason as a natural catastrophe. Terrorist actions are reduced to mere acts of irrational violence with no political significance whatsoever. In fact, according to Debord's definition, even the immediate experience of threat is transformed into the polished, routine representation of death. Covered bodies of victims or a line drawn by the police where the body lay is both more frightening and more acceptable to a Western eye. The death is absent but it can be imagined, and as such it fully corresponds to the cliché. This amalgamation of all terrorist acts into a single formula, the absence of actors, the enclosure into one pre-fixed image, the enormous, specifically-designed courts and prisons – all aim at the separation of terrorists from 'ordinary' and sane people. Even funerals in 'normal' graveyards became problematic.[21] But, at the same time, the whole spectacular machinery gives terrorists an incredible and quite undeserved importance, publicity which they on their own could never dream of acquiring.

With the passage of time, terrorists lose their image as moral deviants along with their contact with the social base. Their ideology weakens and the existence of the group is threatened. This can be the consequence of a clandestine existence, of lack of cohesion within the group, of more efficient police or of the fact that other terrorist groups enter the 'market'. But, provided with free access to the media, and aware of the effect that their actions have had so far, terrorists develop a sort of 'spectacular' self-consciousness. The clan-destine group becomes a mirror image of the state. Just as the state spectacularises itself when it is weak, so do the terror-ists. But, according to Jean Baudrillard, terrorism as a global spectacle reflects its society, too. 'Silent majorities' or the inert masses are, according to the French philosopher, capable of absorbing and emanating anything – even terrorism. The important thing is to maintain the status quo. The third phase of terrorism is thus a pure competition between the two 'spectacular monsters': uniforms, splendid and fascinating machine-guns, show-trials, and extraordinary measures of protection on the one hand; absolutely senseless but logisti-cally impressive kidnappings and assassinations on the other. As the years go by, the 'impersonal' state and 'human' terror-ists might even reverse their roles. The terrorist act exploits the traditional role-based identity; an attack on a function, rather than on a person, signals that all those who occupy the same function may sooner or later become victims. But in the process of martyrdom, attacked civil servants suddenly become people – the judge killed as a judge and appreciated for his whole life only as a functionary, turns into a vulner-able man with a wife and two children. The state acquires a human face. Terrorists, on the other hand, tend to turn their own fallen comrades into a myth. Their commitment to the 'cause' is the only virtue worth mentioning. Those who die for the cause are 'divine'[22] and inaccessible heroes. The ter-rorists themselves fall into the trap of self-spectacularisation, which at one time had been a despised characteristic of the state.

Terrorism as a Substitute for State Spectacularity

The social benefits of spectacularisation are primarily linked to the way in which the terrorism is presented. They do not determine when the spectacularisation will start. Here, time becomes a crucial point in the analysis of political responses to terrorism. The spectacularisation of terrorism should not be confused with the 'invention' or 'fabrication' of enemies, even though it rarely corresponds with the actual threat. The origins of terrorism lie elsewhere in waves of social protests, in the disintegration of extra-parliamentary groups and in the rigidity of political systems. The violence, however benign in comparison with that which succeeds it, is taken as a given when the spectacularisation starts. The Red Brigades were formed in 1969 and initiated their actions in 1971, but nobody in Italy saw terrorism as a threat until 1975. Therefore, the problem is not only why the threat was exaggerated, but also why the threat was not perceived when it was already there. The following discussion analyses the relationship between the lack of state spectacularity, the need for a public consensus, and terrorism as a potentially spectacular phenomenon.

Occupying the same public realm and therefore dependent on the same public, diffuse theatricality (festivals, carnivals and social movements) and state spectacularity (usually in the form of ceremonies, celebrations and parades) have often overlapped in their history. Often they have fiercely competed with one another. The state, with an ever-present desire to absorb and co-opt festivity, and festivity, as a constant gestural challenge to the state and the established world order, could only find equilibrium within the institutional theatre. The theatre was often used as a unique and ultimate buffer in the constant fight between spectacularity and theatricality. But there are also moments when the theatre is unable to bridge the gap between the two forms, e.g., when the official ideology and traditional foundations of the society are threatened, and popular support of the regime is indispensable for its survival. In such a case, political power structures have an increased propensity to spectacularise themselves or provide some other form of 'show' for their vast and hungry audience. All forms of diffuse, spontaneous theatricality are then absorbed or institutionalised, and oppositional theatre is marginalised. It probably happened in the twilight of the Roman Empire (decline of the theatre, absorption of popular rituals by the state, insistence on spectacular games); at the end of the Middle Ages (when the church, despite its dislike of the idea of theatre, transformed festival activities into religious spectacle); and, in a much more perverted form, in most of the recent paranoid regimes, from Fascism to Stalinism. On the other hand, the collapse of the spectacular state might lead to an increase in the importance of the institutional theatre and/or diffuse theatricality. In any case, the spectacular state (or any other predominant power) has always been one of the most important and efficient means of suppressing dissent and eliciting public support. The hegemony over the public realm is thereby equally important as the hegemony over violence.

Among three European states affected by left-wing terrorism in the seventies, only France could still build up its spectacularity on the legacy of the Gaullist idea of grandeur, the charismatic aura of its Presidents and the false but convincing theme of its 'spotless' and revolutionary past. Two other countries, Italy and Germany, endowed with the pre-war tradition of not only high but exaggerated spectacularity, lost all of their symbolic power after the war. If the national myth and the leader are the last harbours of state spectacularity in democratic states, Italy and Germany were historically deprived of using either.[23] But this lack was neither obvious nor important so long as political systems were polarised. Extremism allowed political parties to step in and develop their own spectacularity and/or theatricality, incarnated in party festivals, congresses and demonstrations. Yet, in the period of transition from a 'centrifugal' towards a 'centripetal' political system, this void became apparent, and the 'state's absorption of society' became necessary. The power competition in centripetal systems takes place at the centre of the political spectrum and not at the extremes. Since extremist activists are shut out, centripetal systems are known to be susceptible to dissent and highly dependent on public consensus. Thus, the transition coincided with, or even provoked, the series of upheavals in Italy and Germany. The pressure to create wide public consensus within centripetal political systems forced Italy and Germany to look for a substitute for their own crippling state spectacularity. Since terrorism could function as a 'myth which can be used for purposes of social control . . . and increasing social solidarity',[24] it became a major unifying force in these two countries throughout the whole difficult period of transition.

It should not be surprising, then, that the only country which went through the terrorist hurricane in the seventies and could afford to keep silent about it was France. Close observation of the facts reveals that the deaths caused by terrorist attacks in France were close in numbers to those that occurred in Germany and that the potential of clandestine groups was far greater. For instance in only one month – July, 1974 – the group called GARI committed twenty-four bombings all over France,[25] something that no group ever managed to do in Germany or Italy. But, thanks to the police, who treated them as common criminals and not ideological enemies, the terrorists were put in jail even before they themselves could decide who they were – another phenomenon unknown in Italy or Germany. The suppression of the facts was so successful that even serious scholars, not to mention the French themselves, were absolutely convinced that there was no left-wing terrorism in France during the seventies.[26] This silence can only be explained by the fact that France, although there was nothing spectacular about her politics in the seventies, did not *need* terrorism at the time. France was living through the years of full political polarisation; the state still had the means to develop its own spectacularity and it was much more profitable to rely on the old 'fraternité, liberté, égalité' propaganda than to insist on internal bogeymen. In 'occupied Europe' France played at being a human rights oasis, announcing all the leftist and even terrorist refugees that it had accepted, but never mentioning those who were expelled.[27] Police counter-terrorist efficiency was concealed by overt statements such as 'only monstrous societies can give birth to monsters',[28] and France evidently refused to see herself in such company.

Spectacularisation of terrorism, though, did exist but it was the spectacularisation of *other* nations' terrorism. This was used as one more proof of France's 'diversity', 'prestige' and 'divinity' in world affairs – the essence of the old Gaullist idea of the grandeur and spectacularity of the French state.

Conclusion – Costs of Spectacularisation

Regardless of occasional apocalyptic visions and warnings typical the *fin de siècle* atmosphere, the Western world is once again self-content and self-assured. Optimism, deeply ingrained in Occidental culture, swept away the doubts and the traumas of the seventies. Visible and invisible victims tend to be forgotten, political mistakes pardoned. Mass society has supposedly dissolved into the self-proclaimed postmodernism. In the absorption of social and political tensions which exploded in left-wing terrorism, spectacularity, not for the first time in history, played an important role.

The main problem with left-wing terrorism was not how to handle it technically. The example of France proves that it could have been done in a more efficient and less visible way. The main problem was how to face it and accept the fact that it was neither a hallucination nor an invention of media, politicians or society. The only thing which could have been done, once the terrorism was already there, was to present it in such a way that it started working for and not against society.

The essence of spectacularity is frivolity, and it should not be regarded as a vice. Or the contrary, if something is presented as a spectacle then it is presented in a bearable form. The spectacle is a surrogate. Instead of seeing the real death, instead of confronting something dangerous and different, instead of experiencing a real horror, the audience is faced with a far more pleasant substitute.

But this surrogate is double-faced and has its costs. Terrorism itself can also be understood as surrogate – a surrogate for revolution. Reduced to a violent performance, it was apparently more dangerous, but at the same time invisibly more potent and ingenious. Instead of realising how mediocre the terrorists' proposals were for the new society, people were fascinated with their romanticism. Instead of realising that they were killing benevolent political figures, the audience was impressed with the logistics of their actions. Terrorists' sympathisers did not respond to their call for universal revolution. But the silent consensus which the terrorists acquired was just as disproportionate to their activities as the exaggeration of the terrorist threat. Fascinated with the image, many thought that the revolution would really come from the 'barrel of a gun'. The lowest number of strikes ever registered in Italy was in 1978, the year of the highest level of violence. The official explanation is that this was due to the workers' solidarity with the government. Perhaps. But it is also possible that it was a result of the wait-and-see attitude, of the hope that omnipotent and omnipresent terrorists would change an immobile Italian political system.[29]

Let us conclude with Guy Debord. 'In the really inverted world, the truth is the moment of the false.'[30] In the inverted world of spectacle, the truth and the falsity of terrorism were doomed to be misplaced.

NOTES

1. See *La Reppublica*, 28 April 1988, 2.
2. See, for instance, Alex P. Schmid and Janny de Graaf, *Violence as Communication: Insurgent Terrorism and the Western News Media* (London: Sage, 1982) or Franco Ferrarotti, *L'Ipnosi della violenza* (Milano: Rizzoli, 1980).
3. This is a summary of Franco Ferrarotti's argument in 'Quale il ruolo dei mass media verso il terrorismo' in *Terrorismo Internazionale* (Rome: Adnkronos, 1987). Ferrarotti was one of the main advocates of the total information black-out during the Moro Affair.
4. I have in mind the terrorism which has developed in the last years in Lebanon, Ethiopia and Chad. The kidnappings of technicians, engineers and other 'unimportant' people are rarely reported since the governments concerned either enter into secret negotiations with the terrorists or are unwilling to negotiate at all (i.e. to protect their citizens). The publicity is obviously undesirable in both cases. Yet there is no sign that this kind of 'invisible' terrorism will soon come to a halt. On the other hand, David Rapaport, for instance, argues that religious terrorism rejects publicity. Since religious terrorists communicate with the deity, not with secular power, they despise attention. See Rapaport, 'Terrorism in Three Religious Traditions', *American Political Science Review* 78, no. 3 (September 1984): 660-678.
5. This is an excerpt from Guy Debord's *Spectacular Society* published in 1967 and one of the mandatory readings in 1968. It is quoted according to 'Il nuovo dittatore, lo Stato-spettacolo' in *L'Espresso*, supplement to no. 3 (25 January 1988): 62-3.
6. See Luigi Allegri, *Teatro e spettacolo nel Medioevo* (Milano: Biblioteca Universale Rizzoli, 1988).
7. See Michael D. Bristol, *Carnival in Theatre* (New York: Methuen, 1985) and Michail Bachtin *L'oeuvre de Francois*

*Rabelais et la culture populaire au Moyen Age et sous la Renais-
ance* (Paris: Gallimard, 1965).

8. See Yves M. Bercé, *Festa e rivolta* (Cosenza: Pellegrini editore, 1985).

9. Rapaport, *op. cit.*, 660.

10. Phil Cerny, 'Non-Terrorism and the Politics of Repressive Tolerance', in Phil Cerny, ed., *Social Movements and Protests in France* (London: Frances Pinter, 1982), 94-5.

11. Ibid., 94.

12. See Hannah Arendt, *The Human Condition* (Garden City, NY: Doubleday & Co., 1959).

13. See, for Germany, *Analysen zum Terrorismus* (Opladen: Westdeutscher Verlag, 1981-1984) and, for Italy, Nando dalla Chiesa, 'Sessantotto e terrorismo' in *Il Mulino*, Bologna, no. 273 (January/February, 1981): 53-95.

14. See Jean-Paul Sartre, *Sartre in the Seventies* (London: Andre Deutsch Ltd., 1978).

15. See Herbert Marcuse, *Counterrevolution and Revolt* (Boston: Beacon Press, 1972).

16. Renato Curcio, 'La cultura come meccanismo di produzione, circolazione e fissazione dell'informazione extra-genetica', *Corrispondenza internazionale*, Rome, nos. 20-2 (July 1981-February 1982): 100.

17. The only study known to me is Donatella della Porta and Sidney Tarrow, 'Unwanted Children', *European Journal of Political Research*, 14, nos. 5-6 (1986).

18. Michael Bommi Baumann, *Terror or Love* (New York: Grove, 1977).

19. 'Counter-community' is a term used by Ronald Tiersky to explain the persistence of sect-like Communist Parties in Western Europe. See R. Tiersky, *Ordinary Stalinism* (Boston: Allen Unwin, 1985).

20. The Meinhof photograph evidently served as an inspiration for Heinrich Böll in *The Lost Honour of Katharine Blum* (Harmondsworth: Penguin, 1975).

21. In 1977, huge protests preceded the funerals of Stammheim prisoners in Stuttgart. The Mayor of Stuttgart had to intervene and protect the rights of citizens – terrorists or non-terrorists – to be buried according to their last wishes and the desires of their families.

22. 'Those who die for Ireland have no need of prayer' is one of the IRA's slogans.

23. For an excellent analysis of Italian post-war spectacularity see Piero Leone, *Lo spettacolo della politica* (Cosenza: Editoriale Bios, 1987). Leone's position is that a) spectacularity is neither 'bad' nor 'good', but necessary for the modern state and b) that Italy as a state has only recently – in the period when Craxi became Prime Minister – acquired

spectacularity. In other words, Leone is also of the opinion that the Italian state lacked spectacularity in the period in which we are interested – the second half of the seventies.

24. Cerny, *op. cit.*, 95.
25. See Alain Hamon and Jean-Charles Marchand, *Action directe* (Paris: Seuil, 1986).
26. Phil Cerny stated that there was no real terrorism in France throughout the seventies and that the groups which existed were, rather, 'pseudo-terrorist' (*op. cit.*, 115).
27. Unless forced to, as in the case of Klaus Croisssant, defence lawyer of the Baader–Meinhof group, whose extradition to Germany provoked mass protests in France.
28. This statement published by *Le Monde* in the days of the Stammheim Affair, October 1977, created a diplomatic scandal between Germany and France.
28. Italian workers were neither thrilled with the government of 'national solidarity' formed after the Moro kidnapping, nor extremely sympathetic about Moro's personal tragedy. See Erica Robin Wagner-Pacifici, *The Moro Morality Play: Terrorism as Social Drama* (Chicago: University of Chicago Press, 1986).
30. Debord, *op. cit.*, 95.

4

Aspects of Terrorism in the Work of
Piscator and Brecht

MICHAEL PATTERSON

Despite Walter Laqueur's warning that 'a definition [of terrorism] does not exist nor will it be found in the foreseeable future',[1] it is nevertheless possible to identify certain constituent elements of the term. *The Blackwell Encyclopaedia of Political Thought* describes terrorism as 'A form of political violence, directed at government but often involving ordinary citizens, whose aim is to create a climate of fear in which the aims of the terrorists will be granted by the government in question'.[2] The UK Prevention of Terrorism Act 1976 s.14 (1) speaks of 'the use of violence for political ends [including] any use of violence for the purpose of putting the public in fear'.

From these descriptions, three aspects of terrorism may be distinguished. First, terrorism must involve violent activity, at least the destruction of property and, more likely, the killing of people. Mere preparedness for violence in the event of a revolution or commitment to a policy of violence without oneself participating in it are not in themselves sufficient to attract the designation of 'terrorist'. Second, this violent activity must be informed by a political ideology, however perverted that ideology might appear to an outsider. Random violence without political motivation is not terrorism. Whatever else he may have been, Charles Manson was not a 'terrorist'. Third, although 'terrorism' originally referred to government by the use of terror, as in the French Reign of Terror, in modern parlance terrorist activity is always conceived of as being directed towards a change in the status quo and is therefore targeted on the authorities of a state and is aimed at those who support existing regimes, even at 'ordinary citizens' who may only offer tacit consent to the continuing rule of the authorities.

All three elements must be present at the same time to constitute terrorism. Violent activity coupled with political ideology has characterised many armies throughout history. Violent activity including attacks on the authorities might be typical of any band of criminals. Political ideology plus the demand for radical change informs any revolutionary movement. But neither the Crusaders, the Mafia, nor the Irish nationalist organisation, Sinn Fein, whatever one's feelings about them may be, were or are terrorists in the modern sense of the word.

In some ways, terrorism is an ideal topic for modern drama. It readily embraces spectacular action, political debate, and personal conflict, and allows members of an audience insight into an area of contemporary society that is both hidden from them and yet potentially relevant to their lives.

I propose here to examine the ways in which the two most renowned exponents of twentieth-century political drama, Piscator and Brecht, approached the subject of terrorism in their theatre work. To do this I shall look at two contrasting pieces: the first, Piscator's only excursion into the staging of a classic; the second, the play that, according to Brecht, pointed most decisively towards the future of the theatre. I refer to Piscator's 1926 production of Schiller's *The Robbers* and to Brecht's 1930 *Lehrstück*, *The Measures Taken*.

Friedrich Schiller wrote *The Robbers* (*Die Räuber*) in 1780 while still at school, and it bears many of the hallmarks not only of Schiller's own adolescence but also of the so-called *Sturm und Drang* literary period. Written heavily under the influence of Shakespeare, who had but recently replaced Corneille and Racine as models for the German theatre, *The Robbers* boasts an untidy, rambling, melodramatic plot. It contains forged letters, disguised messengers, two sons (one noble, the other villainous), and an old father who, like Gloucester in *King Lear*, is deceived into believing that his good son has betrayed him and that his evil son loves him. It is a piece full of powerful rhetoric and philosophical utterances. Its extreme emotionalism sometimes lapses into banality. It is hard to imagine, for example, how the false report of the death of the noble son,

Karl, could be received with anything other than hilarity:
'A bullet shattered his right hand, so he took the standard
in the left. . . . I found him on the evening of the battle sunk
beneath the rain of bullets. With his left hand he staunched
the spurting blood; he had buried his right hand in the
earth.'³

When Brecht attended a performance of *The Robbers* at a
Trade Union gathering in 1920, he too saw only its melodramatic qualities. However, Schiller was an inspiration to
the first group of systematic terrorists in the modern sense,
the *Narodnaya Volya*, who assassinated Tsar Alexander II on 1
March 1881. At their first convention in Lipetsk in June 1879
they declared that they would 'fight with the means employed
by William Tell',⁴ a direct reference to Schiller's play of 1804.
And *The Robbers*, over two centuries old, might make a fair
claim to being the first in world theatre to deal with the
subject of terrorism. A play like *Julius Caesar* does indeed
show an assassination through conspiracy and the violent
overthrow of a regime, but Brutus leads an officers' coup,
not a terrorist group. Similarly, the many Christian-martyr
dramas of the Spanish Golden Age or of French Classicism
hardly qualify, since their heroes, though subversive, are also
totally non-violent. In *The Robbers*, however, one may detect
all three elements of terrorism outlined above. The action
is unquestionably violent, including the burning of a town
and the rape of nuns in a convent. The robber band also
clearly operates outside the law and seeks to destroy those
in power. The only area where it is doubtful whether one
may properly speak of terrorism here is that of ideology.
It is questionable whether the hero's motives are political
or in fact personal. Certainly, Karl Moor is concerned to
use violence in the cause of justice, not merely to achieve
wealth:

> He doesn't murder in order to rob the way we do –
> he doesn't seem to bother with the money. . . . But
> if he were to get hold of a landowner who treats his
> peasants like cattle, or a villain with gold trimmings
> who corrupts the law and blinds the eye of justice with
> bribes, or any other of their little lordships in their fine
> array – my God, then he's in his element and carries on

like the devil, as though every fibre of his being were a fury.[5]

Karl himself sums it up in the following words: 'I am no thief that conspires with sleep and midnight . . . my work is retribution – vengeance is my trade.'[6]

Despite this 'Robin Hood' motif of righting the wrongs of an unjust world, it is undeniable that Karl Moor's motivation to oppose authority originates primarily in his apparent rejection by his father and not from any coherent political ideology. He does indeed oppose injustice, but sets himself up as absolute ruler over his own robber band and treats his followers with contempt. His pseudo-political utterances are vague and idealistic, and cannot form the basis of any serious revolutionary programme. His credibility as a terrorist is also further undermined by his wavering commitment. He is repeatedly attacked by an overactive conscience, at one point confessing, 'You can make a mistake – believe me, what seems strength of mind may turn out to be despair.'[7]

After successfully storming his ancestral home, Moor effectively causes the death of his father and brother and then kills his sweetheart on the somewhat dubious grounds that he is no longer worthy of her. Finally, he surrenders himself to the authorities by delivering himself into the hands of a man who will collect the reward on his head and so be able to feed his eleven children. Despite certain characteristics that may reasonably support the claim that *The Robbers* is the first play in world theatre to deal with terrorism, it is undeniable that the main thrust of the piece is the revelation through melodramatic episodes of the personal fate of an essentially unpolitical character.

When, in 1926, Leopold Jessner invited Piscator to direct at the prestigious Staatliches Schauspielhaus in Berlin, Piscator decided to stage a classic. This was to some extent an acknowledgment of the valuable spadework which Jessner had already done in presenting the classics in a manner relevant to modern audiences. Before Jessner, the plays of Shakespeare, or of Schiller and Goethe, were staged as museum-pieces, as pretexts for historical pageantry or, as with Max Reinhardt's productions, as the opportunity for exploring 'universal truths' in an effectively theatrical manner. When, as a result of the

upheavals after the First World War, Jessner was appointed
Director of the theatre formerly belonging to the Kaiser himself, he opened in 1919 with a production of Schiller's *William
Tell* in which he presented the Swiss struggle for national liberation as a comment on the modern Germany's achievement
in overthrowing the rule of the Kaiser. The critic Ihering
called the production the 'cultural visiting-card' of the Weimar
Republic. Understandably, both traditionalists who wanted
their Schiller performed against pretty Alpine backdrops, and
right-wing elements who despised anything that celebrated
the new Republic were outraged. The first performance was
brought to a halt by jeering, and while the actor playing Tell
remonstrated with the audience, the police were called to
restore order.

Modernising the classics – not just putting Hamlet in dinner-
jacket and bow-tie, but seriously attempting to discover for a
contemporary audience the relevance of a work of the past –
had become a vogue. It was a process which Brecht, who had
himself staged his own version of Marlowe's *Edward II* in 1924,
was later to call *Aneignung* (appropriation). Jessner himself
staged Shakespeare's *Richard III* as a warning of the dangers
of dictatorship in 1920, and, after Piscator's staging of *The
Robbers*, he produced *Hamlet* in 1926, using the court setting as
an obvious reference to the Germany of the recent past, with
Claudius clearly suggesting Kaiser Wilhelm. Another director,
Erich Ziegel, had already staged *The Robbers* in modern dress
in 1921, complete with steel helmets, 98-mm cannon and red
flags.

However, Piscator's approach was much more radical than
Ziegel's. He first cut the text heavily, removing much of the
philosophical debate, reducing the melodramatic content and
eradicating some of the minor characters. His boldest move,
however, was to turn the anarchist villain of the robber-band,
Spiegelberg, into the hero of the piece. Piscator wrote about
this adaptation in his *Political Theatre*:

> Spiegelberg . . . was my dramatic gimmick, my regulator,
> my barometer. I had the 'nerve' to use this little man to
> test whether Karl Moor might not perhaps be a romantic
> fool and the gang of brigands around him simply robbers
> in the most straightforward sense of the word . . . and not

communists at all. . . . It is curious how serious this little man became, true Schillerian villain that he is . . . – he, the man who had no real father in a lordly palace in the background, who was no handsome, tenor-voiced hero, who had none of the attributes of the 'beloved' leader! . . . He unmasked Schiller's pathos, he unmasked the ideological weakness of the background, but he did honor to the dramatist by coming alive for a modern audience – he alone – while the world which surrounds him is dead.[9]

In order to make his point, Piscator costumed Spiegelberg in a Chaplinesque outfit, complete with cane and bowler (Chaplin's *The Gold Rush* was the sensation of the Berlin cinema that year), and Spiegelberg's face was made up as Trotsky, 'an ambitious Jewish intellectual, speaking with sober pathos', as the critic Kurt Pinthus described him.[10] Thus, combining the detachment of the clown with the acumen of the revolutionary politician, Spiegelberg provided a foil against which the idealistic utterances of Karl Moor could be set.

An example of this is provided by the scene in which Spiegelberg persuades Moor's companions to become robbers. For Schiller this was a piece of villainy and the source of Karl Moor's tragedy, for he is thereby prompted to do evil as surely as Macbeth is tempted by the witches. In Piscator's version, Spiegelberg raises the consciousness of the dispossessed proletarians (attired in work-clothes and cloth caps), and urges them to violent, but politically directed, action. In effect, Piscator's Spiegelberg turns Schiller's robbers into a terrorist group.

Piscator's stage-directions recorded in the prompt-copy[11] reveal the emphasis that he wishes to place on this conversion to a life of violent crime. Spiegelberg is required to speak to the gang 'as if to children, irritating slightly by his certainty', then 'tragically, with appealing humour, quietly smiling.' As his eloquence succeeds, 'the others all have this smile – they have got over their despair, the scene is touching.' As Hugh Rorrison puts it: 'The men are workers, proletarians, Spiegelberg is their spokesman, he is no longer vile and devious but sympathetic and persuasive.' Predictably, Spiegelberg

is here deeply disappointed by the men's decision to appoint
Karl Moor as their leader, but not, as in Schiller's original,
merely from a sense of thwarted ambition but because they
will now be led by a man acting from personal and highly
idealised motives rather than from a true sense of political
purpose.

Spiegelberg's death also undergoes a significant change in
Piscator's version. In Schiller his envy and frustration at being
led by a man of high moral principles induces him to persuade
a fellow robber, Razmann, to steal up on Karl Moor and murder him. It is simply a plan of personal revenge, an attempt to
assert his own leadership over the robber band. Piscator's version, which still contains much of Schiller's actual text, reads
as follows:

> SPIEGELBERG [to Razmann]: Yes, things must change,
> if you're the man I always took you for, Razmann! I
> clearly see how things must change. He has gone missing
> – they think he's almost lost – Razmann – I think his final
> hour has come, eh? Not even a flush in your cheeks to
> hear the freedom bell tolling? Haven't you the courage
> to understand a bold hint?

> SCHWEIZER [angrily drawing his dagger]: You swine!
> [Stabs him dead. Sixth verse of the Robbers' Song, almost whis-
> pered but rhythmic. Spiegelberg's death, a fantastic death, he
> dances while the Robbers sing – all the grotesque tragedy which
> Schiller revealed in him is shown in this dance].

> SPIEGELBERG [while the Robbers sing]: Bondman of a
> slave. Political infants! The freedom bell! [Seventh verse
> loud, almost wailing, then a long pause, while Spiegelberg dies
> downstage with the knife in his breast. At the moment of death
> he stares into the distance. The Internationale.]

In Piscator's version, Spiegelberg's death is that of a communist visionary. The desire for personal revenge is replaced
by a call for freedom, and the singing of the Internationale
puts the seal on the nobility of his vision. It must also be
noted that in many ways the ecstatic cries about the freedom bell and the sentimental pull of music as Spiegelberg
dies contain much of the kind of pathos that Piscator was

purporting to eliminate from Schiller, a point I shall return to later.

In other ways too, Piscator's production of *The Robbers* emphasised the political aspects of the piece. In Schiller, Karl Moor's home is a Gothic castle ruled over by his frail father until the latter is incarcerated by the villainous son Franz. For Piscator, Traugott Müller designed a set reminiscent of Eisenstein's *Battleship Potemkin*, which had just opened in Berlin. The Moor castle now became a fortress bristling with guns, ruled over by an energetic and autocratic count ('fresh, fit and in high spirits', as the prompt-book describes him). Thus, when the robber band storms the castle in act 5, this appears as a revolutionary act, and the play ends, not with Karl Moor 'giving himself up to the police' but with cries of 'Freedom! Freedom!'.

Piscator's attempt to appropriate Schiller's play as a contribution towards class struggle, his re-evaluation of the figures of Karl Moor and Spiegelberg, and his elevation of a band of robbers to a group of proto-communist revolutionaries, predictably met with severe disapproval from several quarters. As Piscator reported in *The Political Theatre*, Bernhard Diebold felt that this modernisation of the classics was a mistaken undertaking:

> [O]ne cannot deep-freeze warm classics as Piscator has done; what is required are not variants of Coriolanus and Karl Moor, altered in form and content until they are aesthetically unrecognizable, but quite simply new plays from new authors. A de-heroified Karl Moor does not give Schiller a new life upon the ruins of himself; when Spiegelberg is made the moral hero, Schiller finally and unquestionably dies the death of the classics. . . . A Spiegelberg drama cannot be derived from Schiller, but must be written anew – say, by Brecht.[12]

Interestingly, Brecht wrote far less about revolutionary groups than is commonly supposed, and to my knowledge he never portrayed terrorists in the sense in which I have defined the word. His first presentation of revolutionaries was of the Spartacists in his early play *Drums in the Night*, premiered in Munich in 1922, but his view of their activities is very sceptical, the protagonist Kragler preferring to take his woman to bed rather than to fight a hopeless revolution. *The Mother* (1932) shows the political education of a simple woman, but there is no suggestion that the revolutionary group of which she becomes a part are committed to a programme of terrorist violence. The sons of Señora Carrar (*The Rifles of Señora Carrar*, 1937) are engaged in violence, but in a civil war and not as terrorists. In *Fear and Misery in the Third Reich* (1938) we encounter resistance groups against Fascism, but again there is no indication that they will pursue anything other than peaceful means. Of his later plays, *The Days of the Commune* (1956) debates the problem of maintaining revolutionary achievement by force and his version of *Antigone* (1948) shows a single individual in determined opposition to a tyrannical regime. But it is in his *Lehrstücke* of the early 1930s that Brecht comes closest to an analysis of the phenomenon of terrorism.

The *Lehrstück*, or 'learning-play', was a new concept in drama, a piece intended to educate the cast more than to entertain an audience. When the most important of them, *The Measures Taken* (*Die Massnahme*) was premiered at the Berlin Philharmonic in December 1930, the so-called 'Control Chorus' was sung by the three thousand workers present. *The Measures Taken* describes the efforts of four Communist agitators, sent from Moscow to a Chinese city to foment revolution. Their efforts are constantly hampered by the over-zealousness of one of their number, the so-called Young Comrade. When his behaviour threatens to destroy their revolutionary efforts, they take the decision, agreed to by the Young Comrade himself, to execute him and throw his body into a lime-pit. Thus, although politically motivated violence forms the climax of the piece, it is violence directed towards a member of the revolutionary group not, as in most forms of terrorism, at the world outside.

One might attempt to extend the concept of terrorism to the use of terror to discipline members of the group. Certainly, it often seems that some terrorist atrocities degenerate into a display of bravado towards one's own followers rather than having any other clear objective. However, the violent death perpetrated on the Young Comrade is a last resort, not a threat that has been held over him. It is only when all efforts to educate him in the hard discipline of Communist Revolution have failed that he is put to death, and this occurs, as I said, with his full acquiescence:

> CONTROL CHORUS: . . . It was not easy to do what was right. It was not you who passed judgment, but reality.
>
> THE FOUR AGITATORS: We shall repeat our last conversation.
>
> THE FIRST AGITATOR: We will ask him whether he agrees, for he was a brave fighter.
>
> THE SECOND AGITATOR: But even if he does not agree, he must disappear, completely.
>
> THE FIRST AGITATOR [to the Young Comrade]: If you are caught, they will shoot you, and since you will be recognised, our work will be betrayed. So we must shoot you and throw you into the lime-pit, so that the lime will burn you up. But we ask you: do you know a way out?
>
> THE YOUNG COMRADE: No.
>
> THE THREE AGITATORS: So we ask you: do you agree?
>
> [Pause.]
>
> THE YOUNG COMRADE: Yes. I see that I have always acted wrongly.
>
> THE THREE AGITATORS: Not always.[13]

The tone is cool and objective, the decision to murder the Young Comrade presented as rational and necessary. But we are entitled to ask just how rational, just how necessary. There is no discussion, as there would be in a realistic piece, of alternative outcomes. It remains unexplained how the removal of their colleague will save the other three men and their revolutionary work. The Agitators have been recognised as foreigners in the city and have only five minutes to reach a decision, since the authorities are close behind them. Will these troops abandon their hot pursuit on finding only three men, or will the elimination of the Young Comrade permit the three others to go underground within five minutes?

Might it not be more expedient to use the Young Comrade as a decoy for the pursuers? These questions are not debated and are probably not meant to be asked. Interestingly, earlier versions of the piece do at least include the possibility of smuggling the Young Comrade back across the frontier, but the version quoted above, which was prepared for the *Collected Works*, does not address this possible outcome. The fact is that the stark and unemotional language of the piece deceives us into thinking that the decision is a purely rational one and we therefore accept its validity, just as surely as the theatre of emotion which Brecht so despised hypnotises our feelings. In one of his earliest pieces on epic theatre, Brecht asserted that the emotions of the spectator would be aroused not because there was no way out for the protagonist, but precisely because there was a way out. Yet here, in the case of the Young Comrade, we are invited to believe that there is no alternative to his gruesome end.

What we may observe here, both in Piscator and in Brecht, is an unfortunate sleight of hand, which claims for political theatre a new clarity in place of the obfuscation of former ages but which itself suffers from a lack of rational debate. In the chapter of his *Political Theatre* dealing with *The Robbers*, Piscator stated that the requirements of Art are 'the conditions of a clear and rational mind.'[14] And yet, as we have seen, while jeering at the naive idealism of Schiller's eighteenth-century hero, Piscator in his handling of Spiegelberg's death hardly offers an object lesson in clarity or reason. Brecht was well aware of the dangers of a pseudo-revolution in the theatre: 'The passion which [actors] showed when their stage-wives were unfaithful is now shown by them when the stage-capitalist reduces wages. The public is no longer in suspense whether Romeo gets Juliet but whether the proletariat gets the power.'[15]

In 1955 Ernst Schumacher, the East German critic, expressed his suspicion of Piscator's brand of theatre: 'It was the involvement of the spectator in the action, the removal of the division between theatre and reality, such as Piscator strived for, which made the theatrical illusion total. The spectator was not allowed to think clearly.'[16]

Brecht, however, did indeed make a much more serious

attempt to change not only the content but also the form and reception of modern theatre. And yet, as we have seen, in some of his more didactic works he was anything but the sage philosopher of the stage that he purported to be. He spoke of his own manipulation most clearly when he argued: 'To prevent the audience from 'swooning away', to combat 'free' association, small choruses can be placed in the auditorium to show them the right attitude, to invite them to form their opinions, to summon their experience to their aid, to exercise control.'[17] As John Peter drily comments: 'It is hard to understand from this unpleasant passage, how on the one hand you combat free association in people's minds, and at the same time invite them to form their own opinion. But Brecht's intention is quite clear: he is proposing to use the theatre for purposes of direct persuasion.'[18]

What we may observe here, then, is a curious phenomenon. Two of the most highly regarded figures of political theatre of the twentieth century only tangentially deal with the problems of achieving revolution by violence.[19] More disturbingly, both men share certain characteristics of terrorism in their own theatre work. For, like terrorists, in the guise of rational political action they operate in a way that is not open to discussion. In theatrical terms, the death of Spiegelberg or the killing of the Young Comrade offer as little political discussion as one may have with the car-bomb or the taking of hostages. Piscator does not condemn Karl Moor's violence; he is merely dismayed at its lack of genuinely political motivation. Similarly, Brecht rejects the spontaneous humanity of the Young Comrade in favour of the cold and murderous discipline of the Party. The acquiescence of the Young Comrade in his own death and the obliteration of his corpse in the lime-pit sanitise the violence perpetrated on him and make an act of terrorism appear acceptable.

That Piscator and Brecht condoned violence as an instrument of political struggle is understandable, given the immediacy of their need to resist Fascism. That they did so with so little rational argument is disturbing.

NOTES

1. Walter Laqueur, *Terrorism* (London: Weidenfeld & Nicholson, 1977), 5n.
2. David Miller, ed., *The Blackwell Encyclopaedia of Political Thought* (Oxford: Blackwell Reference, 1987), 514.
3. *The Robbers*, act 2, sc. 2.
4. See Laqueur, *op. cit.*, 22.
5. *The Robbers*, act 2, sc. 3.
6. Ibid.
7. Ibid.
8. See Michael Patterson, *The Revolution in German Theatre* (London: Routledge, 1981), 88f.
9. Erwin Piscator, *The Political Theatre*, trans. Hugh Rorrison (London, 1980), 128-9.
10. *8 Uhr Abendblatt*, Berlin, 13 September 1926.
11. Hugh Rorrison, 'Piscator directs Schiller's 'Die Räuber' at the Staatliches Schauspielhaus, Berlin', *Regie in Dokumentation, Forschung und Lehre* (Salzburg, 1975). All quotations from Piscator's prompt-book are taken from this article.
12. Bernhard Diebold, 'Death of the Classics', *Frankfurter Zeitung*, 2 July 1929, cited in *The Political Theatre*, 131-2.
13. *The Measures Taken* (1937/8 version in *Collected Works*), sc. 8.
14. *The Political Theatre*, 134.
15. Bertolt Brecht, 'Die Übernahme des bürgerlichen Theaters', *Schriften zum Theater*, 3:121.
16. Ernst Schumacher, *Die dramatischen Versuche Bertolt Brechts 1918-1933* (Berlin, 1955), 136.
17. Cited in Eric Bentley, *The Playwright as Thinker: A Study of Drama in Modern Times* (New York, 1946), 232. [Slightly adapted.]
18. John Peter, *Vladimir's Carrot. Modern Drama and the Modern Imagination* (London, 1987), 287.
19. It is true that *The Days of the Commune*, at the very end of Brecht's career, debates the problem of preserving the fruits of revolution through force, but this is hardly the same as an analysis of what one would normally term terrorism.

5

Individualist and Collectivist Models of Terrorism in German Expressionist Drama

LADO KRALJ

I

Terrorism, or rather, terrorist violence, was a focal point of the controversies surrounding German Expressionist playwrighting. It appeared not only in the plays that were written but also in the psychological temperament of the writers themselves. At all times, it coloured their relations towards one other and towards the world at large. As drama was the most important of the written Expressionist genres, it contained all the ideological features of Expressionism as a whole, including terrorism. The first part of this essay deals with the fears and the violence emanating from responses to terrorism among playwrights as a group, the second part with the significance of terrorism in the dramatic plots and action of their major works.

Within Expressionism, poetry had a much lower reputation than drama, and drama in turn had much lower status than the paraliterary genre of the manifesto, to which all Expressionist writers turned their hand. For most of the Expressionists, publishing manifestos was an absolute moral duty. How can we explain this strange hierarchy of genres in a movement that was rebellious and subversive? In one sense, it was a strictly political ordering. One must always bear in mind that the Expressionist movement started out as a political phenomenon, that is to say, as a new ideology which was, by turn, critical, militant, utopian, authoritarian and totalitarian. The victory of this new ideology was at all times the writer's main priority. Art was considered to be secondary, and its mission was to enable its ideology to triumph.

The moment literature is denied its autonomy and is treated merely as an aid to ideology, it ceases to be regarded as anything other than functional or utilitarian. This is what happened to literary Expressionism. Energies were channelled into producing manifestos entirely at the service of the movement's ideology. Manifestos preached new ethical values, but would also be the basis for public meetings where they could be read aloud to assembled crowds. Paratheatrical presentation was central to the concept of dramatic effect and stage drama imitated in many ways the public context of the manifesto as a form of communication between speaker and audience. Expressionist ideologues often liked to use special terminology borrowed from Christianity to stress the quasi-religious aspirations and fervour of their new ideals. The theatre was called 'the place of the cult' and drama was termed 'a mission', or more often still, 'an annunciation'. The function of annunciating was so important that the whole of Expressionist drama was often called 'the drama of annunciation', a term used in research to this day.[1] In poetry, annunciation also played a role but a much diminished one, since poetry was not linked to the place of the cult and relied in addition for its sensorial representation almost purely on the spoken word. As for prose, the Expressionist movement could find little use for it. Prose was by its nature too extensive and its power of immediate emotional impact too small to allow it to become a genuine Expressionist genre.[2]

The concept of drama as a mission to annunciate ideas, had a decisive consequence on its form. Expressionist drama gave up the demand for causal logic and plausibility, for unified plot and for empirically-based characters. Instead, it offered a loose structure of 'stations of the mind' that were to be understood in metaphorical terms as moral examples for its audiences to follow. The audience was shown the spiritual pilgrimage of the central protagonist towards his final goal, which was either the purification or the revolution of the mind. The Expressionist drama thus conforms, as Sokel has stated, 'to an "epic" or "narrative" rather than a strictly dramatic pattern'.[3] Instead of a well-knit plot, we find a pageant or pilgrimage-like structure, a loosely-connected series of images or situations. This model was taken over from Strindberg but it can also be traced back to the Christian miracle and passion plays. Brecht, whose early work paralleled that of the Expressionists, adopted the same model and developed it theoretically as an 'epic' theatre. But there was a decisive ideological difference. The Expressionists, as Sokel remarks, 'sought to appeal to the emotions, while Brecht's Epic Theatre tried to appeal to the critical intellect of its audience'.[4]

What exactly were the ideas that the plays were supposed to annunciate to their audiences? The answer is far from simple, since the ideology was never exact or homogeneous. On the contrary, it was full of contradictions and inconsistencies. In origin, the common denominator resided in the spirit of Romanticism, in an atmosphere of extreme subjectivism which in the name of 'genius' defied all the institutions of the social world and especially the German middle-class way of life. We must also bear in mind the unfulfilled hope of the previous generation of Naturalists and Symbolists, the hope that the turn of the century would bring a happier and more humane era to European civilisation. As this, in their eyes, had not happened, the Expressionists reacted with predictable bitterness and frustration, and this became the most common characteristic of their writing. In addition, they had a deep fear of modern life, of the new rapid forms of urbanisation and industrialisation in modern German society. They pessimistically assumed that these were all things with which the individual could not cope and their bitterness transformed itself into a critique of society which managed to be aggressive, self-righteous, authoritarian and self-destructive all at the same time. In the rightful task of destroying existing society in order to build a new and better one, everything was permitted. In conceiving their new world and their new man of the future, however, the Expressionists were notoriously vague. They tended to cling to verbose rhetoric, which was utopian, sentimental, naive and had little concrete basis in contemporary life. They were always against everything, but usually in favour of nothing.

Within German society, the Expressionist movement was socially and culturally marginal. Today, they might well be called a subculture or counter-culture. Their ideas were far

from effective in penetrating a mass audience. Newspaper and
magazine reviewers ignored their work or else treated it with
sarcasm and contempt. The coterie of self-styled prophets who
saw themselves as reaching out to all humanity were in fact
little more than a small group of bohemian intellectuals circu-
lating ideas among each other. From their main watering-hole,
the Café des Westens in Berlin, they promulgated from 1910
onwards their firm belief that the whole of European civilisation was now at an end, stale, static, worn out and moribund.
Any sudden crisis or catastrophe was welcome grist to the
mill. The arrival of Halley's Comet in 1911, for instance, was
awaited with great excitement as it was expected to collide
with the earth, and it motivated Jakob von Hoddis to write
the first Expressionist poem bearing the characteristic title, *The
End of the World*. The Expressionists longed for war, 'even an
unjust one', as Georg Heym put it, if only to destroy the
atmosphere of intolerable and motionless tension, of a 'rotten
and sticky peace'.[5] World War I came as a confirmation of the
wishes and prophecies of many of them. Their actual
experience of it, however, was another matter and many soon
became eager pacifists.

In this atmosphere of discontent, Expressionists felt a moral duty to develop a completely new collective identity. But
this was not an easy task. Expressionist doctrine was sectarian and always in flux. Today's goodness could change
into tomorrow's evil, today's morality into tomorrow's deca-
dence. Staying in tune with the time in order not to be
deemed reactionary by one's fellow cultists was a constant
preoccupation. Communication thus tended to be hysterical,
neurotic and even terrorist. Negativity produced a kind of psychic terrorism. Two memoirs of minor contemporary
Expressionists, those of Friedrich Schulze-Maizier and
Richard Meyer, show something of this atmosphere of psychic
terror. Discussing the ambience of Der Neue Klub, a famous
gathering-place where, among other activities, Expressionist
plays were performed, Schulze-Maizier writes: 'The latent
malice of intellectuals rarely affected me so intimately as it did
in the midst of this . . . highly-gifted Berlin circle. Now and
then it felt as if one had landed in a tribe of headhunters.' Of
the Café des Westens, Meyer writes:

We weren't thinking so much about the intoxicating feeling of getting into print as keeping a watchful eye open
for the possibility of being attacked in words which
could bite like quicklime or sulphuric acid. Incredible
animosity which we had to counter was all around in
the air . . . Had new fronts developed? Was another turncoat to be exposed? What camp threatened to
split? Were ominous creakings to be heard in the tim-
bers of a friendship? Who was winning? Who was
falling?[6]

Expressionist ideology had three main sources: anarchism,
socialism, and the writings of Nietzsche, especially those con-
cerning nihilism. In the *Genealogy of Morals*, Nietzsche had
declared that European culture and civilisation was based on
the false moral principle of a now decaying Christianity. Once
modern man realised that God was dead, the whole system of Christian values collapsed and nihilism resulted. The
Expressionists became attracted to the whole battery of meta-
phors through which Nietzsche tried to illuminate nihilism –
disorientation, twilight, illness, decay, madness, the fall into
the bottomless abyss, and death. They also became attracted
to the alternative he proposed, the affirmation of a strong,
ecstatic will-to-power.

Though ignored by reviewers and treated with indifference by average audiences, Expressionist ideas were closer
to the *Zeitgeist* than either the Expressionists themselves or
their adversaries realized. Despite their eccentric diction, their
belief in instant redemption, their turn to collectivism and
their intolerance of those who did not believe, their advocacy
of terror meant they had produced in their revolution of the
mind all the central features of the new totalitarianism which
was to convulse Europe during the twenties and thirties.
But for them it stayed in the realm of metaphor. To use
Freudian terminology, they were sublimating the political
nightmares of their age by allowing them into consciousness
only through the language of metaphor. For both the Nazis
and the Stalinist communist parties of the period, Expressionism was an unwanted cultural rival too close for political
comfort. In 1933, the Nazis openly burned Expressionist books
while in the same year Georg Lukács, the Hungarian Marxist

critic, wrote a denunciation of the movement in exile in Moscow. For him, the Expressionists were the petit-bourgeois offshoot of a decaying society and, willingly or not, the precursors of Fascism. By publishing his article in the Moscow-based German magazine *Internationale Literatur*, Lukács condoned a form of censorship, analogous to that of book-burning. The Soviet government had just begun accusing Russian Futurism of formalism and decay, and Russian Futurism was the avant-garde twin of German Expressionism.

II

In Expressionist drama, there were two different models of terrorist violence, an individualist one and a collectivist one, the latter following chronologically upon the former. In the former model, which prevailed until just after the beginning of World War I, playwrights would infuse the changing social environment with aspects of the coming nihilism which Nietzsche had predicted. In this environment, the protagonist, 'the young poet' or 'a genius' who is usually a version of the playwright's alter ego, strikes back against an intolerable situation by desperate acts, such as murder or, more specifically, patricide. The killing of the father was a common obsession enshrined in the title of Arnolt Bronnen's play *Patricide* (*Vatermord*, 1922). Here the revolution takes place in the closed circle of the family, since destroying the traditional family was seen as a first step on the road to wider social revolution. After the war the latter, a more collectivist theme became dominant. Here, terror was exerted not on individuals but on the masses by a powerful leader who managed to combine charisma and tyranny. Terror in the hands of the charismatic leader was a means of awakening the masses from apathy and forcing them to search for their true humanity.

One of the most famous of the early plays was Reinhard Sorge's *The Beggar* (*Der Bettler*, 1912). Its subtitle is *A Dramatic Message* and the protagonist is called alternately The Poet, The Son or The Young Man, according to the social situation or the different 'stations' of his pilgrimage. Predictably, he is a genius who writes dramas that are true missions to save the destitute of the earth who, he imagines, would rush to the performances of his plays. Since he cannot finance the staging of his plays, all his work is in vain. His life at home has crumbled as his father, a construction engineer, has long since gone insane. The madness of the father involves a mission to save the world by rearranging its geography and then destroying it with the help of gigantic digging machines, which he had first seen in night visions, on the planet of Mars. On running short of ink to edit his planning blueprints, he stabs his pen into the heart of a captured bird and writes in blood. The figure of the Father stands for a now demented traditional authority, but also embodies the new technology which is a source of trauma for the son. The Poet kills the father with poisoned wine and in the last act we discover him editing the manuscript of the play we have just been watching. His life is his total creation.

In Walter Hasenclaver's *The Son* (*Der Sohn*, 1914), it is the father who is convinced his son has gone mad. Whipped by the Father after his failures at school, the Son becomes suicidal, dreaming of escape from the rich, middle-class home which has become a prison. He succeeds in fleeing and founds 'The League of Youth against the World', whose slogan is 'Death to the Fathers!'. The League's success inaugurates a generational revolution. In the final showdown the Son and Father confront each other with gun and whip but the Father is struck down by a heart attack, horrified by his son's revolutionary fervour. Despite its exaggerated pathos, most Expressionists saw the play as a convincing example of how to annunciate the 'revolution of the mind'. Other plays in the individualist mould go beyond the familial model. The murder by the protagonist may be of someone he sees for the first time in his life, as happens in Paul Kornfeld's *The Seduction* (*Die Verführung*, 1916). The hero's murder of a dull, average and 'soulless' man is a revolt against decay by 'a Man of the Soul' as Kornfeld in his theoretical writings, describes the Expressionist hero. Contemptuous of traditional morals, open to the sensual ecstacies of existence, the Man of the Soul is neurotic and egocentric to the end, oscillating violently between euphoria and despair. Having served his prison sentence for one murder, he tries to commit another, but is killed by the poison he has prepared for his victim. Even in the act of dying, he continues to threaten a vengeful return to plague the world.

After 1914, Expressionist ideology took a decisive turn from individualism to collectivism. Individual and subjective revolt was declared not only unsuitable but reactionary. Many Expressionists felt a moral duty to win over their uncomprehending comrades through friendly persuasion. 'Get active, politically active', was Ludwig Rubiner's advice. The writer should become politically engaged for the benefit of the masses. Johannes Becher called his former colleagues 'poets of decay'. Ernst Toller called unreformed writers 'cowards hiding in waste-paper baskets'. The new ideals combined models of collectivist action with the need for a charismatic leader or redeemer. Walter Hasenclaver suggested that if the Expressionist writer is politically committed, he could well be chosen for this position himself. The element of subjectivity thus returns in effect through the back door, and joins the myth of the Nietzschean Overman to the political model of collective solidarity.

Ernst Toller's play *Masses and Man* (*Masse-Mensch*) is explicitly dedicated 'to the world-revolution' and 'to the proletarians'. He wrote it in 1919 while serving a five-year prison sentence in the fort at Niederschönenfeld for being one of the organisers of the Bavarian Soviet Republic. The term 'human masses' is used exceedingly often in the play's dialogue, and the first two characters in the dramatis personae are 'The Workers' and 'The Women Workers'. Yet the protagonist and antagonist are still individualised characters. These are Sonja Irene L. and the Nameless. Sonja Irene L. is a revolutionary, but bourgeois in terms of her class origin. The Nameless is the charismatic leader of the human masses, proletarian in background. The action takes place during a revolution which appears to be modelled on that of the revolutionary uprisings in Munich and Berlin in 1918–19. The Nameless advocates absolute terror as part of the right of the masses to revenge against their oppressors, a right which works to the benefit of the revolution. He uses his power to ensure a massacre of the prisoners the revolutionaries have taken. At first Sonja Irene L. opposes him, even at the risk of being accused of treason, but eventually she relents and subjects herself to revolutionary discipline. Nevertheless, she feels tremendous guilt and her experience makes her lose her faith in the revolution. The author's moral perspective in this play, and consequently the questions he raises, show very clearly the internal inconsistencies of the Expressionist ideology. It is the dilemma of two opposing slogans, which we might summarize as follows: 'We must love all the people, since we are all brothers', and 'The revolution must win by all means, even by terror, since its victory will bring the New Empire of happiness to everyone.'

The play, *The Nonviolent Ones* (*Die Gewaltlosen*, 1919) by Ludwig Rubiner, on the other hand, annunciates non-violence as the only true means of revolution. Non-violence is advocated by three charismatic leaders and eagerly applied by the masses under their influence. The will-to-nonviolence will conquer, convincing even the most sadistic tyrants and jailers of the need for a new humanity in which all hierarchy and political control will cease to exist. Treachery within the movement, however, hampers the achievements of the revolution. The three leaders decide to exterminate the very idea of leadership by starting with themselves. If all three 'go the way of self-destruction', if they sacrifice their lives publicly, the deed will bring salvation to the masses. The result is that they 'offer' themselves to the angered masses who tear them apart. Instead of being the propagators of terror, they are its recipients. The people are born anew and an age of freedom and solidarity begins. The play shows Expressionist ideology at its most utopian and voluntaristic, where it becomes a purely propagandist construct, cut off from all empirical reality. The author admits in his preface that the characters are representative of ideas and that the play is ahead of its time in his urge to turn desire into reality.

Georg Kaiser was the most prolific and, many would argue, the greatest of the German Expressionist playwrights. His plays have certainly stood the test of time and are almost as easily produced on stage now as when they were first written. The *Gas* trilogy is perhaps the most characteristic of Kaiser's works. The three plays *The Coral* (*Die Koralle*), *Gas I* and *Gas II* (1916–20), concentrate on three generations of the same family and show the life-stories of three main protagonists: the Billionaire, his son and his great-grandson. *Gas II* is a drama of the future in which the state has nationalised the huge gas factory the family had previously owned, and the Billionaire's great-grandson has sunk down the social scale to the lowly position of an ordinary worker. He is called the Billionaire Worker and becomes the charismatic leader of the factory masses during a period of wartime production when energy resources are of vital importance to the war effort. The Billionaire Worker develops a pacifistic programme under the slogan 'Workers of the world, unite!', but enemy soldiers occupy the country and the factory, destroying his internationalist ideals. The Billionaire Worker succeeds, however, in laying his hands on the deadliest weapon the factory has ever produced, a special war gas capable of the wholesale liquidation of opponents. The workers urge him to use it against their enemies but the Billionaire Worker persists in his pacifism. As he cannot persuade the workers to build 'the empire that is not of this world', an empire of peace and tolerance, he finally decides upon the catastrophic annihilation of friend and foe alike. The play ends in apocalyptic horror.

III

If the anarchic rebel is the hero of the first Expressionist period the charismatic leader is the hero of the second. Both are moralizing extremists who wish to change the world. Both are deeply implicated in both the actual and symbolic aspects of terror. Both act out a kind of utopian drama which badly misfires. Yet the collectivist model of drama is one which transposes the anarchic rebel into a position of institutional power through charisma, and this is the connecting link. At the same time, it is what makes the leader's relationship to the masses so questionable. Whereas the anarchic rebel finds ignorance rife among the middle-classes, the charismatic leader finds it to be widespread in the proletarian masses who must be forced to change, to open their eyes, to come to some kind of awareness. They must be transformed from object into subject, by looking beyond their immediate material needs. The charismatic leader, however, is only able to offer a programme for the future in which material problems are transferred onto the plane of moralism. The leader's vision is mythic and utopian. Therefore, his most central function, the 'salvation' he offers his people, is also the most questionable. This is precisely where terror returns with a vengeance. The anarchic rebel advocates improving the world through individual murder, but the desperation of the charismatic leader turns the desire for change into terroristic massacre. In Rubiner's play, this essentially amounts to the rebel's terror being used against himself, while the end of Kaiser's trilogy demonstrates the breakdown of all utopian dreams of happiness and the triumph of catastrophe.

NOTES

1. See Eberhard Lammert, 'Das expressionistische Verkündigungsdrama', in Hans Steffen, ed., *Der deutsche Expressionismus: Formen und Gestalten* (Göttingen, 1970).
2. See Albert Soergel, *Dichtung und Dichter der Zeit. Neue Folge: Im Banne des Expressionismus* (Leipzig, 1927), 796.
3. Walter H. Sokel, *Anthology of German Expressionist Drama* (New York, 1963), xx.
4. Ibid., xxi.
5. See Gerhard P. Knapp, *Die Literatur des deutschen Expressionismus: Einführung, Bestandsaufnahme, Kritik* (Munich, 1979), 30, 35.
6. Cited by Richard Sheppard in 'German Expressionism', in Malcolm Bradbury and James MacFarlane, eds., *Modernism* (Harmondsworth: Penguin, 1978), 281.

PART II

Contemporary Drama

6

State Terror and Dramatic Countermeasures

MARY KAREN DAHL

> When I was a prisoner in Germany in 1940, I wrote, staged, and acted in a Christmas play which, while pulling wool over the eyes of the German censor by means of simple symbols, was addressed to my fellow prisoners. . . . [O]n this occasion, as I addressed my comrades across the footlights, speaking to them of their state as prisoners, I suddenly saw them so remarkably silent and attentive, I realized what theatre ought to be – a great collective, religious phenomenon.
>
> Jean-Paul Sartre, 'Forgers of Myth'

> I was in Cracow for a new production of *Hamlet*. When the line 'something is rotten in the state of Denmark' was uttered onstage, a murmur rippled through the audience from the gallery – right under the ceiling to the first row in the orchestra. When, later, the line 'Denmark's a prison' was repeated three times, I felt the house go silent, like the sudden lull before a storm. Then applause broke somewhere in the center of the auditorium, and then somewhere in the gallery: individual, quiet applause that seemed frightened at its own audacity. In another moment the entire auditorium had broken into a fierce applause that lasted until hands went numb.
>
> Jan Kott, *Theater of Essence*

Sometimes by the playwright's design, sometimes by a kind of spontaneous combustion, citizen resistance to state oppression takes shape in the theatre. That this is so is clear from the witness of Sartre, who was imprisoned by the Nazis, and of Kott, who in the 1950s was a theatre critic in Poland.[1] Why it should be so is not entirely evident.

The everyday attributes of theatre make it a difficult form to use when critiquing the state. Because it is a public art, performance texts and players are subject to controls of various kinds. Lack of performance space, lack of funding, sparse audiences, public criticism, censorship, harassment, arrest,

exile, or imprisonment – none of these risks is far-fetched. The
single amateur performance of Vaclav Havel's 1975 revision
of John Gay's eighteenth-century play, *The Beggar's Opera*, for
example, took place under Czech police surveillance. 'Most of
those who had come to see the production were then interrogated and some lost their jobs as a result.'[2] In March, 1988,
Waldemar Fydrych, leader of a pro-Solidarity guerrilla theatre
troupe, the 'Orange Alternative', was arrested for staging
a street protest against the installation of new Soviet missiles
in Poland. He was released only after 'dozens of Polish artists
and intellectuals, including the film director Andzej Wajda
appealed' his imprisonment.[3] Given the practical difficulties
and real dangers, why use a medium like theatre to attack
a repressive state? Does something about the form (other
than the obvious fact that theatre people do theatre in pref-
erence to doing anything else) make it uniquely worth the
attempt?

   This question prompts a second commonsense observation.
Theatre is not just public, it is communal. Since the time of
Aeschylus, the performance space has been a place in which
a people collectively articulates, examines, redefines, reorders
and reaffirms its values. The 'communal nature' of theatre
is foregrounded when we think about the dynamic in the
audience during those remarkable moments Kott describes
at the Cracow production of *Hamlet*. First one, then another,
and finally all members of the audience joined in repudiating
Stalinism. Those moments represented the spontaneous creation of meaning by a community of spectators, watching and
reinterpreting the performance text to fit their own lives. For
those moments, spectators united in expressing values held in
common – values they would rarely put into words for fear of
reprisals.[4]

   If, however, we are to think about how theatrical performance might respond to state terror, we need to look at the
outlines of the terrorist state itself. Walter Laqueur provides a
point of departure: State terror, he asserts, like individual terrorism, 'aim[s] at inducing a state of fear among the "enemy".'
More particularly, state terror involves 'acts of terror carried
out by governments against their own population, including
systematic intimidation, arrests, killings and other means of

coercion. This is usually directed against political opponents, but it can also affect sections of the population considered "objectively" harmful, and it has been, on occasion, altogether indiscriminate,'[5]

Hitler's Final Solution to the Jewish question, Stalin's purges, the Argentine Junta's 'disappearances', the South Korean regime's torture of opposition leader Kim Keun Tae all give flesh to Laqueur's definition, But the mechanics of state terror is still undescribed. And it is in the mechanics of terror that we may discover theatre's potential response, At a conference at Stanford University in February, 1988, Professor Ulrich K. Preuss noted that, according to some schools of political theory, the legitimacy of government derives from the freely-given consent of the governed. (This notion is explicit in the Constitution of the United States, for example.) Preuss theorised that terrorist states invert this relationship. The terrorist state, like other states, holds a monopoly of violence. But, unlike other states, the terrorist state uses violence against its own people to 'force obedience' to its rule and its rules, In effect, by exercising violence, the state tries to force the populace to internalise the values that perpetuate its existence and its mode of operation. Consent is not freely given; an attempt is made to exact it from the governed.

Preuss suggested that the effect of state terror is to create in the people (or some portion of them) a feeling akin to the 'Stockholm Syndrome' noted by psychologists in hostage situations: that is, the victims of violence come to identify with their captors, who are their potential executioners. In fact, a terrorist state requires a homogeneous society. This desired homogeneity is based, in some degree, on the internalisation of common values: dissent and dissenters are the enemy. Or, as Preuss says, 'political dissent is value dissent.' Maintaining the necessary homogeneity requires constant affirmation of the state's values and constant 'suppression' of dissent.

The role of violence in suppressing dissent in a fully developed terrorist state is clear: Violence is used by the state

> to authenticate the validity and effectiveness of the common values and the identity of the value community by

defining, fighting against and extinguishing its foes. It is essential for the fulfilment of this function that violence be exercised in public. This ensues from the particularities of violence: violence is mute, . . . it is efficient, that is, it depends only on minimal social or cultural contexts in order to reach its aim to create physical or psychic harm and anguish; that is why it is intelligible to all. . . . [I]ntegration into the 'value community' is not mediated through conviction, persuasion or other complicated processes of communication but through a 'language' which is understood spontaneously by everybody: physical force.[6]

In other words, the state forces into being a false community. It forces community through violence. For the individuals who make up this false 'value community', Preuss's analysis suggests that at least two different kinds of surrender may be involved. The first is at a superficial level and reflects a very natural fear of pain and what we often call the survival instinct: one must be seen to comply with orders in the hope of ensuring physical safety. At a second level, there is a kind of surrender that involves 'buying into' the value structure: one adapts to the status quo and develops rationalisations that allow one to cooperate with or actively support the state and its terrorist methods.

Preuss's hypotheses about the 'value community' and the role violence plays in creating and enforcing that community suggest areas in which theatre intersects with state terrorism. Theatre, too, acts on individuals at the levels where values are created and affirmed. In a terrorist state, therefore, theatre has the potential to affirm values that distinguish victims and potential victims of the state from the rest of the populace. Theatre may bind together the opposition – the community of victims and their supporters – so that they can resist the dominant structure of terror.

Three playtexts that attempt to create or affirm a dissident community are Dario Fo's *Accidental Death of an Anarchist*, Ronald Harwood's *The Deliberate Death of a Polish Priest*, and Athol Fugard's *Statements After an Arrest Under the Immorality Act*. In each, the playwright explicitly appropriates, then subverts, the texts or formal structures of the regime he critiques.

And in each case, performance of the text provokes questions about the nature and efficacy of political theatre.

Dario Fo wrote *Accidental Death of an Anarchist* as a response to a specific event in a particular social and political context. On 12 December 1969, seventeen people were killed and approximately one hundred wounded when a bomb exploded in the Piazza Fontana in downtown Milan. The bombing occasioned large-scale repression of political activists on the extraparliamentary left (students, labour organisers, workers) throughout Italy. In the immediate aftermath of the bombing, the police questioned Giuseppe Pinelli, a railroad worker from Milan, and an anarchist. After three days of interrogation, Pinelli mysteriously fell from a fourth-storey window to his death. Officials called the death a suicide. The courts declined to indict those responsible, but it seemed clear that Italian police had 'accidentally' killed Pinelli. Moreover, right-wing fascists, not left-wing anarchists, had planted the bomb.[7]

According to some observers (including Dario Fo), a recently elected Christian Democratic government had attempted what might be called a political scapegoating. Police officials blamed Pinelli for the bombing; once he was dead, they could close the case and use the threat of more anarchist bombs to consolidate their control of the government. They expected the country to unite behind their policy, which was to repress the left-wing opposition.[8] Instead, public opinion demanded inquiries into the bombing and Pinelli's 'defenestration'. The information revealed by various court cases and investigations was disseminated via performances of Fo's Play. *Accidental Death of an Anarchist* retold the story of Pinelli's death. It corrected the state version so that a true history came to be known by the dissident community. 'In the spring of 1970', Fo explained, 'the comrades who came to see our plays urged us to write a full-length play about the Milan bombs and the murder of Pinelli, discussing their causes and political consequences. The reason for this was the fearful vacuum of information about the problem.'[9] Fo set out to create a source of facts independent of state-controlled information providers.

Fo called the play 'an exercise in counterinformation'.

He explained the technique as follows: 'Using authentic documents – and complete transcripts of the investigations carried out by the various judges as well as police reports – we turned the logic and the truth of the facts on [their] head,'[10] This then was the strategy – to use the texts created by the state in the process of conducting its business as usual to comment on and condemn that business and its associates, who included the clergy, the judiciary, the police and other security forces.

In effect, the play reversed the state's attempt to make Pinelli a scapegoat. The scapegoat was transformed into a martyr for the political opposition, even though Fo celebrated that martyrdom through the device of a comic maniac exploring an official cover-up. When the play was originally produced in Italy, those who wanted merely to be entertained, those who wanted to know what had happened in the Pinelli affair, and those who suspected that the official version was untrue would have gathered for performances. Fo remembers that public as having comprised 'Progressive students, workers, but also, large numbers of the lower middle classes'.[11] The play's revised history of the murder educated the concerned public and bound it together more meaningfully by providing a common history of the event. Again, in Fo's words: 'In the daily debates which took place after performances it was the public itself which jogged us towards greater clarity about the new struggles which were growing daily and developing throughout the country.'[12]

Here Fo is referring to the audience discussions (sometimes called the 'third act') that he and the company regularly used to include spectators in whatever discourse had begun onstage. Tony Mitchell reports that sessions concluding performances of *Accidental Death* usually focused on questions of political strategy.[13] If Mitchell's report is accurate, then the discussions invigorated the public in rather concrete ways: first, they raised the level of audience involvement with the material treated in the performance text; second, they encouraged individuals to think personally about political action and change; and third, they increased the solidarity of the audiences. Speaking up at an event of this kind amounts to relinquishing anonymity and stepping into the public, political arena. This in itself is an act of trust and commitment. Indeed, merely showing up at such an event can constitute a political act, as those interrogated for attending Havel's version of *The Beggar's Opera* can testify.

Fo's experience illustrates how theatre can work to generate values to be held in common by a community gathered for a performance. It also forcibly reminds us of the obvious limitations of theatre noted above. Fo recalls that, even in parliamentary Italy, he and his troupe 'were subjected to provocation and persecution of all kinds, sometimes more grotesque and comical in their repressive stupidity than the very farce we were performing'. Mitchell is more specific: he mentions bomb threats and police searches before audience members were allowed into performance sites.[14] To avoid such difficulties, playtexts may necessarily be performed beyond reach of the regime.

The Deliberate Death of a Polish Priest, presented in London in October 1985, focuses on another political murder. In October 1984, Father Jerzy Popieluszko was abducted and murdered by members of the Polish Interior Ministry. South African playwright Ronald Harwood based his documentary drama on transcripts from the trial of the four officers directly responsible. The play details the kidnapping and murder in the words of those who planned and perpetrated it.[15]

There are many points of correspondence between *Deliberate Death* and *Accidental Death of an Anarchist*. Harwood's play, like Fo's, retells a true story about recent political events. The two stories run along similar lines. In each, a member of a dissident community is killed (accidentally, it is claimed) by members of the state police/security force; the murder is part of the state's programmatic intimidation of dissidents. In both cases, the murders caused sufficient public outcry that official investigations were conducted. These investigations are the targets of the two plays, each of which shows the investigation in question to have been compromised. In addition, the two plays are structured as investigations of investigations. Fo stages a mock re-enactment of a judge/auditor's inquiry. Harwood documents the historical trial of those accused of the priest's murder. The priest's driver, who was kidnapped with him, comments on the trial's progress and outcome. His commentary serves a function similar to the comic antics of Fo's maniac: that is, it increases the spectator's ironic distance. And finally, each play appropriates information developed and disseminated by the relevant state's investigators. The information is then used to subvert the authority of the actual investigating institution.

In the early 1980s, *Accidental Death of an Anarchist* was playing in London's West End. The textual reference between Harwood's and Fo's titles is striking, and the list of parallels between the two plays suggests a purposeful restructuring by Harwood of Fo's politico-theatrical concept. Such a dialogue transcends the boundaries of a single theatrical event. Ideas and values can evolve in the space between events, so that the scope of the discussion is enlarged. This is a politicised, energised use of the phenomenon Umberto Eco talked about as unlimited semiosis, whereby all things 'modify' (or reverberate against) all others. In this particular case, Harwood seems to be responding to Fo's invitation to consider or debate political strategies. Indeed, Harwood proposes his own model of exemplary action: Popiełuszko's Christlike, non-violent activism that resists an oppressive regime even unto death.

Harwood presents us with a good example of the power of theatre to affect audience opinion. His play is built on religious themes, and invokes all the iconography associated with Christ to draw us in. It reads as a hand extended to those who have been, or will again be, imprisoned for solidarity's sake, especially for those who, like Adam Michnik, have chosen with Popiełusko a politics of nonviolence.[16]

Although theatre can be said to create and affirm an audience-as-community in opposition to the false community of state terror, plays critical of a regime might never be seen by the community most immediately concerned. Thus, the texts of Vaclav Havel's plays circulated in *Edice Petlice*, a Czech samizdat, and were widely read, but, after 1968, the plays were performed only in translation abroad. Is it possible for such performances to have benefitted the subject dissident community?

Limited gains are sometimes apparent. For example, the success of the 1973–74 Royal Court, London, productions of the three *Statements* plays is said to have protected playwright Athol Fugard and his collaborators, black actors John Kani and Winston Ntshona, even within the borders of South Africa. Moreover, once the plays had been seen abroad, it became possible to publish the playtexts without fear of censorship.[17]

Greater gains are difficult to describe and impossible to measure. But those most resistant to articulation, such as the interior component of theatrical experience, are the most important to recognise. With that in mind, let me offer one spectator's response to the third of the *Statements* plays, Fugard's *Statements After an Arrest Under the Immorality Act*, and its affirmation of anti-apartheid values.

The play concerns two lovers – the woman, white; the man, black – who are betrayed to the South African police for their violation of laws against miscegenation. The play opens just after they have completed an act of lovemaking. Their arrest is re-enacted, and a policeman reads the statements taken at that time. While the events are fictive, the play originated in an actual 'image of six police photographs of a White woman and a Coloured man caught in the act. . . .'[18] Thus this play, like those by Fo and Harwood, uses the forms of power to critique the regime in power.

Visually, *Statements After an Arrest* progresses from dim into bright light. Often this pattern signifies redemption or apotheosis. Here the reverse is true. The darkness with which the play opens is a place of trust and comfortable intimacy, where voluntary self-disclosure is possible. Both the man and the woman are naked. The woman talks about drying her hair in the sun, the colour and smell of the day, the sound of doves and bees in the heat. We as spectators are included in the sphere of intimacy and trust.

The arresting officers bring with them harsh, unrelenting light. They train their flashlights on the lovers as they scuttle around the room trying to find clothes, or cover of any kind. Voluntary self-disclosure is now replaced by involuntary, compulsive exposure and self-incrimination. The fear is preconditioned. Each simply starts talking. They describe how

they met, who they are, and what they feel without any overt
interrogation taking place. The light is hellish, unbearable,
emblematic of the unrelenting scrutiny of the state, which
penetrates every private place, the body's every crevice. The
man and woman disintegrate before us. The two are sundered
one from another. 'All of me that found you must now lose
you', the Woman says.[19] Each individually fragments. The
man's final speech, delivered as he stands naked except for
his vest, translates the emotional and psychological process
into concrete terms:

> [God] wants back what is left. . . . I give him my feet
> and my legs, I give him my head and body, I give him
> my arms, until at last there is nothing left, just my hands,
> and they are empty. But he takes them back too. And then
> there is only the emptiness left. But he doesn't want that.
> Because it's me. It's all that is left of me.   They arrest it
> all the same.[20]

And all the while, we watch. Or, more to the point, I watch.

The final image of Fugard's play is of Lear's bare forked
animal, unaccommodated man, on the barren heath the state
has created. The most private and intimate aspects of two living beings and their relationship are opened to public scrutiny
and judgement.[21] The exposure violates the individual, and
is intended to do so. As a spectator I am forced to participate
in the invasion. Unless I refuse to watch, I become a guilty
voyeur. My only exoneration must be by way of revulsion
against the state that practices such violations.

The movement from plural to personal, from we to I, reflects
the obvious: It is I who, in the midst of a crowd, perceives
and reacts. Indeed, prompted by Fugard's text, I am subject to
rapidly resonating, multiple responses. I am first drawn into
identifying with this man and woman. As the viewer, however, I become a victim myself, angered at being manipulated
into watching this staged representation of what should be a
private agony. The victimisers are the characters who hold
the torches, surrogates for a state that shames me through
our common white skin, and the playwright and actors who
have prepared this discomfort. And yet, like the figures who
aim the torches, I am protected in the dark, privileged to direct
my gaze where I will.

By turns, I am one with the victims, victimised as a spectator, victimiser as long as I continue to watch. Sympathy, anger, and guilt combine to force a radical reassessment of values – and subsequently, of everyday actions. This is the remarkable achievement of Fugard's play.

When one sees how the performance event can engage the individual spectator at the level of his or her material reality, one begins to see ways in which theatre might be used to counter state terror. The shift in register from we to I thus marks a shift in critical stance that is essential to articulating the proposition towards which this argument tends. State terror depends on the reception of a terrorised community. As noted earlier, violence is mute and makes mute. The playwright responds to the state by opposing its message in the theatre. The spectator in the theatre responds both to the state and to the dramatist who speaks back to the state via a text aimed at the spectating community. That community is itself in constant danger of suppression as a consequence of its group and public nature.

It is possible, however, that the very act of perceiving contains within it the seeds of resistence. Rolf Grimminger argues that, when reading, 'the participant engages in a psychic, monologic process that is removed from or even opposed to social action. But in this involvement the individual inevitably affirms "the ethos of inner freedom." . . . "The protest is already included in the process of communication itself, in the retreat to the ego." '[22] Grimminger's thesis applies equally well to spectatorship. It recognises the tension between social action and subjective response, and suggests that even when the import of a staged scene cannot be admitted or stated publicly, the individual spectator can in fact silently appropriate signs to his or her own ends. The special advantage theatre has over reading is that these silent appropriations, or acts of resistence, can be committed in a body, and they may from time to time escape silence and erupt into social action. Violence may attempt to remake the world in its own mute image, but theatre allows us to talk back.

120   Mary Karen Dahl

NOTES

1. The epigraphs are from the following texts: Jean-Paul
   Sartre, 'Forgers of Myth', in *Sartre on Theatre* (New York:
   Random House, 1976), 39; Jan Kott, *The Theater of Essence*
   (Evanston, Ill.: Northwestern University Press, 1984),
   209-10. Sartre's play was *Bariona or Son of Thunder*, trans.
   Richard McLearly, in *The Writings of Jean-Paul Sartre*, eds.
   Michel Contat and Michel Rybalka (Evanston, Ill.: Northwestern University Press, 1974), Vol. II.
2. Marketa Goetz-Stankiewicz, *The Silenced Theatre: Czech
   Playwrights Without a Stage* (Toronto: University of Toronto Press, 1979), 67. The performance was in Horní Počer-
   nice on 1 November 1975. Havel himself has been imprisoned a number of times for his activity with Charter 77,
   most recently in January 1989.
3. John Tagliabue, *New York Times*, 14 June 1988, Section B,
   1-2. The examples of Fydrych and Havel are taken from
   only a small geographic area. For examples from Argentina
   see John Simpson and Jana Bennett, *The Disappeared and
   the Mothers of the Plaza* (New York: St. Martin's Press,
   1985), chs. 1, 12. From New Dehli comes a report of the
   beating death of Safdar Hashmi, director of a street theatre
   troupe, who was set upon by a mob for refusing to stop
   a performance supporting a candidate in a local election.
   Sanjoy Hazarika, *New York Times*, 4 January 1989, Section
   A, 1, 5.
4. Khrushchev's 'secret speech' denouncing Stalin's personality cult and excesses occurred at the 20th Party Congress,
   24-25 February 1956. The performance Kott describes took
   place in late September, 1956. He called his review 'Hamlet
   after the XXth Congress' *The Theater of Essence*, 210.
5. Walter Laqueur, *The Age of Terrorism* (Boston: Little,
   Brown, 1987), 146.
6. Ulrich K. Preuss, 'Legal Representations of Terrorism'.
   Paper presented at the conference Talking Terrorism:
   Ideologies and Paradigms in a Postmodern World, February 1988, at Stanford University, Palo Alto, California. Pas-
   sages paraphrased and quoted are from the unpublished
   typescript, 5-7.
7. Suzanne Cowan gives the figures of 12 killed and 88
   wounded. 'Dario Fo, Politics and Satire: An Introduction
   to *Accidental Death of an Anarchist*', *Theater* 10 (Spring, 1979):
   9-10. Tony Mitchell gives the figures of 17 killed and
   100 wounded. *Dario Fo: People's Court Jester* (London:
   Methuen, 1984), 59.
8. Mitchell describes the 'strategy of tension' as one in which
   'the new Christian Democrat government, having deposed

the centre-left coalition, tried to crack down on the left and dissipate its forces.' *Court Jester*, 59.

9. Quoted by Mitchell from p. 111 of the unpublished MS of his translation of the play in *Court Jester*, 59. The 'comrades' in question, according to Eugene van Erven, were Pinelli's lawyers, who 'decided to collaborate closely on the project: the lawyers would go to court in the mornings and report to Fo in the early afternoon. The playwright would then incorporate the latest findings in the evening's performance even before the newspapers got hold of the information. In this way, the play continued to develop over the eight-year period that it took the Italian legal system to condemn the three fascists who were really responsible for the bank bombing.' *Radical People's Theatre* (Bloomington and Indianapolis: Indiana University Press, 1988), 135.

10. Dario Fo, Introduction, *Accidental Death of an Anarchist*, trans. Gillian Hanna, adapted by Gavin Richards (London: Pluto Press, 1980), iii. Henceforth cited as Fo, Introd.

11. Fo, Introd., iii.

12. Fo, Introd., iv.

13. Mitchell, *Court Jester*, 65.

14. Fo, Introd., iv; Mitchell, *Court Jester*, 63.

15. Ronald Harwood, *The Deliberate Death of a Polish Priest* (New York: Applause Theatre Book Pub., 1985).

16. Adam Michnik, *Letters from Prison and Other Essays*, trans. Maya Latynski (Berkeley: University of California Press, 1985), 76-99.

17. Dennis Walder, *Athol Fugard*, Grove Press Modern Dramatists, ser. eds. Bruce King and Adele King (New York: Grove Press, 1985), 77.

18. Athol Fugard, Introduction, *Statements*, including *Sizwe Bansi is Dead* and *The Island* by Athol Fugard, John Kani, and Winston Ntoshona, and *Statements After an Arrest Under the Immorality Act* by Athol Fugard (New York: Theatre Communications Group, 1986), xi. For Fugard's comments on the evolution of the plays, see *Notebooks: 1960-1977*, ed. Mary Benson (London: Faber and Faber, 1983), 184-203, *passim*.

19. Athol Fugard, *Statements After an Arrest*, 105.

20. *Statements After an Arrest*, 108.

21. That my response is not unique is confirmed by Russell Vandenbroucke, who makes a similar point in nearly identical terms. See *Truths the Hand Can Touch: The Theatre of Athol Fugard* (New York: Theatre Communications Group, 1985), 139.

22. Quoted by Robert C. Holub in *Reception Theory: A Critical Introduction* (London: Methuen, 1984), 116. Double

quotes mark Holub's direct translation; single, his para-
phrase of the original. For the complete argument see
Rolf Grimminger, 'Abriss einer Theorie der literarischen
Kommunikation', *Linguistik und Didaktik*, 3, no. 4 (1972):
277-93; and 4, no. 1 (1973): 1-15, 115-16. For the passage
quoted, see p. 5. I am indebted to Robert E. Innis for
acquainting me with this source and for his many other
insightful suggestions.

7

Utopianism and Terror in Contemporary Drama: The Plays of Dušan Jovanović

DRAGAN KLAIĆ

For the last several decades the concept of utopia has been, with good reason, caught in the crossfire of many different enemies – political scientists and politicians, artists and literati, futurologists and ideologists – all of whom have been in fierce competition to discredit the utopian vision.[1] The past has been de-utopianised. Practically all the great utopias, from Plato's through More's to the predictive narratives of the nineteenth century have been re-examined and found to be faulty in discourses that speak of state terror and not of happy communal life, that outline the oppression of monotony rather than the freedom and tolerance of a creative atmosphere of equality.[2] The future has been de-utopianised as well, especially since the Bomb, the very existence of which poses the threat of total annihilation, making utopian ideas seem superfluous, if not absurd. Hence a sceptical view of the future has emerged that excludes uptopianising and sees behind every technological innovation and social change a new form of oppression, a new cause for alarm.[3]

Against the background of a fierce critique and rejection of utopia, the contemporary terrorist appears as the ultimate utopian, the last believer in dreams no one wants to take seriously any longer. With a zeal similar to that of medieval millennarians,[4] contemporary terrorists aim for the immediate achievement of their far-reaching projects of social change. The terrorist is a utopian in a hurry who is willing to deploy all means, including those of arbitrary, non-discriminatory violence, to realise his utopian plans. Recourse to terror dooms these plans to failure in the short-term and usually pushes

123

their possible implementation into a more remote future. On the other hand, adherence to utopia and sincere utopianism cannot redeem the terrorists nor secure a moral justification for their deeds. Terrorism is a non-selective manner of utopian praxis that misfires. Unavoidably, it turns out to be counter-productive since it tends to bring about unexpected dystopian consequences[5] – as Schiller sensed while writing the paradigmatic *Sturm und Drang* play, *The Robbers* (*Die Räuber*, 1780).

The etiology of the more recent intermeshing of utopianism and terror might be sought in the *événements* of 1968, when there was among young people, and especially students, a sudden surge of utopian energy, an explosion of utopian praxis, carried out more in a histrionic than a violent manner, but quickly defeated and diffused by the reaction of pragmatic politics, using cooptation and repression as carrot and stick. In the ensuing passivity and disappointment, quite a few utopian terrorists were recruited among the hard-core adherents of the 1968 movement in Western Europe and in both Americas.[6]

The contemporary dramatists who sought to formulate and evaluate this process in their plays could benefit very little from such illustrious predecessors as Brecht, who in his *The Measures Taken* (*Die Massnahme*, 1929) used the dense *Lehrstück* formula to proclaim from the standpoint of Stalinist orthodoxy, the unavoidable defeat of sentimental utopianising by pragmatic Party terror. Even Michel de Ghelderode's *Pantagleize*, written in the same year as Brecht's 'leaflet in a dramatic form', has little to offer in its vaudeville format because its clownish naif, turned revolutionary terrorist *'malgré lui'*, never reaches the slightest understanding of the political violence he inadvertently triggers and by which he must perish. While creative solutions to encapsulate the recent fusion of utopianism and terrorism offered by such authors as Edward Bond (especially in his *Lear*, 1971) and Heiner Müller (in *The Task* [*Der Auftrag*, 1970], for instance) are well-known explorations of their Yugoslav colleague Dušan Jovanović (b. 1939), pursued in the same thematic orbit, have not till now attracted much critical attention outside his own country.

I

While Jovanović's dramatic constructs are derived from particular Yugoslav circumstances, they indicate a choice of effective strategies available to any contemporary playwright who
aims to address the issues of politically inspired violence.
Here, self-conscious theatricalism, role-playing and various
allegorical devices anchor a political discourse within an elaborate theatrical metaphor, yet also delineate an ideological
context for utopianism and terrorism. By such means the
author hopes to transcend the dry rationalism of the drama of
ideas (on a Sartrean model, for instance) and the melodramatic
duels of martyrs and executioners. Equally, he hopes to dis-
card the argumentative mode of playwriting inaugurated by
the optimistic spirit of the Enlightenment, and the trite dialectic of goals and means that, within the particular thematic
corpus of radical social change, has been plaguing playwrights
from Schiller to Hauptmann and from Brecht to Bond and even
beyond.

The diffusion of the 1968 revolt into a self-defeating rage,
and into a manipulated revolution that was doomed to fail and
end in a new conformism, was shown in the early Jovanović's
play *The Madmen* (*Norci*, 1969). At the time it was perceived as
an exercise in ludism, i.e., playfulness for its own sake, rather
than as an anticipatory vision of almost prophetic value.[7] The
misunderstanding continued with the reception of his next
drama, *Play out of a Tumour in the Brain, or Polluting the Air*
(*Igrajte tumor v glavi ali onesnaženje zraka*, 1971/72).[8] Seemingly,
this is a play about conflicts *within* and surrounding the theatrical community in a tradition well-known since Aristophanes,
Beaumont, Molière, Fielding and Goldoni, and continued in
our century through the plays of Bulgakov, Giraudoux and
Grass.[9] The satiric elements are concentrated in the first act,
situated in the newsroom of a daily paper, where the journalists attempt to figure out what is happening in the local
repertory theatre. Apparently, the self-styled avant-gardists
in the ensemble have expelled their more traditionalist colleagues and barricaded themselves in the theatre building.
Rumours about their activities spread and the occupation of
the theatre quickly acquires political importance. The author

engineers a satire of both the journalistic and theatrical pro-
fessions and of the political mechanisms set up to white-
wash the event. These developments reflect the conflicts that
shook the Slovenian culture in the 1960s, when the traditional
models of national institutions, and especially theatre, were
revealed as exhausted and obsolete while the conservative
elites attempted, sometimes in a repressive manner, to prevent an alternative culture from constituting itself.[10] When
Jovanović was writing his play, these sharp conflicts were
about to be resolved, but they were still freshly imprinted in
the memory of the Slovenian and Yugoslav public at the time
of its premiere at the Slovenian Popular Theatre in Celje in
1976 and influenced its reception.[11]

The satiric perspective of the play fades with the second act,
as the reporter Križnik and the police inspector Levstik sneak
into the theatre where they find an euphoric avant-garde
group busy with its exercises. For the malaise of a conservative national theatre, the director Dular and his dramaturg
Palčič proscribe a cure that summarises all the platitudes and
worn-out myths of the avant-garde theatre of the 1960s: the
stress on the process rather than on the result, the forceful
merger of the performers and the public, emotional unity
instead of the coherent exposé of ideas, mystical catharsis,
collective ecstasy, expanded consciousness, abandonment of
textual language for the language of the body and melodic,
onomatopoeic sounds.

There is an ample room for satire here, but the perspective is
not satiric at all. The author avoids pejorative or ironic touches.
Instead, he deepens the initial conflict between the modernists
and the traditionalists, which had already resulted in violence,
with a second-level conflict between the theoretical, pseudo-
scientific approach of the dramaturg and the mystical method
of the director. The utopian project of the avant-garde nucleus
has been split into opposing, incompatible utopian schemes,
shaped by two charismatic personalities and enforced with
increased reliance on violence, on the manipulation of the
actors and on the help of the primitive, authoritarian person-
nel of the theatre.

The theatrical institution is turned at first into a commune,
an experimental laboratory, an exile from the world, where

utopias can be built around the idea of a total theatre. Soon, however, it is transformed into an asylum, a mini-concentration camp, a torture chamber, where the leaders terrorise the followers, the different factions fight with one another and the leader of the expelled traditionalists, a famous actor, shoots his enemies at random with a rifle from the cat-walk. The intended utopia is increasingly entangled in manipulative schemes and violent rituals amidst an atmosphere of threat and lunacy. The journalist and the police inspector lose their viewpoint of detached observation. They are drawn into the ensuing havoc and the less they are able to discern what is going on, the more they find themselves involved in esoteric exercises. Some other external power centre seems to run the show in the occupied theatre building, but neither the investigative reporter nor the police inspector can see through all the fog of experimentation.

A quest for utopia turns into a horror show whose conspiratorial logic is diffused by interventions of fantasy. Action loses coherence and the rejection of traditional roles by the part of the ensemble leads to the unconscious assumption of another set of roles, frenetic and increasingly disarticulated, worn as sombre masks of an impenetrable meta-show. Avant-gardism, barricaded in the theatre to pursue its utopian vocation, is nevertheless contaminated from the outside and quickly exhausted inside. The polluted air of society poisons the enclave of experimentation and betrays its expectations of self-sufficiency, making the actors victims of terror from the outside and of terrorism from the inside. The theatrical, even ritualistic facade cannot hide the violent, oppressive nature of this rebellion-become-compliance. While the initial point of rejection is clear – actors stand up against an ossified cultural institution and its assigned role as a shrine of national culture – the ultimate point of defeat is less clear. While the pattern of victimisation is amply demonstrated throughout the action, its ultimate authors and masters remain undisclosed.

Considered beyond the immediate references to Slovenian cultural conflicts, Jovanović's play shows with an anticipatory imagination the development of the avant-garde theatre of the sixties, the *cul-de-sac* of the utopian quest for togetherness, closeness, oneness. The spectacular form of a backstage show synthesises the series of fallacies, crushed hopes and misdirected energies consummated in what Jan Kott has called 'the end of the impossible theater'.[12] In this sense, Jovanović's *Tumour* is a dramatic postscript to the 1960s and to their characteristic brand of theatre, written before the era was in fact truly over or before we could notice that it was over and with what kind of an outcome.

II

In 1979 Jovanović wrote a new play, *Karamazovs*, that dealt in a direct, straightforward manner with the traumatic events of recent Yugoslav history – Tito's break with Stalin in 1948, the emergence of Yugoslavia's independent brand of socialism and the treatment of Yugoslav Stalinists by the authorities at home. Because of the moral and political credit earned in the liberation war, Tito and the Communist Party enjoyed a broad popular support in the ideological dispute with Moscow. Under a strong external threat to national security, which included economic and military pressure and a virulent propaganda campaign by the USSR and the neighbouring 'people's democracies', Yugoslav authorities put all of Stalin's sympathisers in a camp on a rocky northern Adriatic island, called Goli otok, and exposed them to a harsh 're-education campaign'. Here already-converted inmates brutally fought for the hearts and minds of those freshly arrived. Many communists of long standing, partisan war-veterans and high officials were among those arrested, but not all of them were fanatical Stalinists or potential traitors: some were confused by the political shift and unable to grasp the significance of a doctrinal dispute since they were trained to show complete loyalty to Stalin and the USSR; some were slow to prove their support to the new party line; and some were completely innocent victims of denunciations or of police zeal.[13] While the ideological and political conflict that exploded in 1948 determined the evolution of the Yugoslav system in the following decades, the drama of Goli otok was for many years shrouded in silence. The prisoners were released in the early 1950s and most of them were subsequently reintegrated into Yugoslav society. The issue of their administrative incarceration and of methods deployed in the camp remained for decades outside public scrutiny, however.

Jovanović's play pierced a long-standing taboo and aimed to address the difficult moral aspects of the Goli otok episode face on. Previously, in films and literary works, there had been passing allusions to people who suddenly disappeared in the turbulent years 1948–51, some to reappear only years later, as broken men. *Karamazovs*, by contrast, had in the centre of the action an ex-partisan and a devoted communist who contributes with enthusiasm to the socialist construction of the post-war years, works as a journalist and rebuilds his private life – only to be swept away by the Yugoslav/Soviet rift, which he perceives as a catastrophic event, a world suddenly turned upside down. He receives the new set of truths and ideological tenets with incredulity and revolt. He is arrested, made to give up his doubts and accept the position of the Yugoslav Party. He is finally released as a rehabilitated man, but dies as soon as he comes to freedom. The play's action proceeds to show the guilt under which his three sons grow up as misfits who cannot shape their own identities, pursued by the memory of their father's political crime. A father who has sinned (against his party and against his country) and his three sons, who carry this sin as their own burden, is the only analogy with Dostoevsky's novel.

The author's aim was neither to exculpate the Stalinists nor to criticise the anti-Stalinist policy of the government, as implemented on Goli otok, but rather to construct a situation of tragic proportions, where a human being is caught in a web of crushing circumstances that overwhelm his cognitive powers. The simplistic hero/villain opposition is transcended as both the arrested journalist and his fellow-detainee, who is to earn his own freedom by reforming him, are pulled by larger forces beyond their influence and ultimately united in the acceptance of a world view imposed from the above. They are both victimised by ideologically inspired terror because they were believers in the utopia of a single international communist movement, seen as a harmonious brotherhood of just fighters run from Moscow and embodied in the cult of Stalin. Because of his adherence to this utopia the main character pushes aside other values, such as his family or the independence of his country which refused to become a Soviet satellite. The re-education is, in fact, a systematic breaking-down of this utopia, achieved mainly through psychological pressure, a kind of brainwashing, an exorcism of ideological dogma followed by political instruction and various tests of role-playing to prove a newly-felt loyalty to the anti-Stalinist position of the Yugoslav Party.

The mental denudation of the detainee as he is force-fed a whole new belief system overwhelms the fate of his sons in the second part of Jovanović's play. Moreover, because the subject of Goli otok had been hushed up for a long time, the reception of Karamazovs focused on the factual nature of the events in the play and not on the question of whether they were worthy of tragic treatment.[14] The role terror plays in the transformation of a shattered utopia into a reconstituted ideology was by and large overlooked by the public, interested primarily in setting the historical record straight. However, Karamazovs eliminated the taboo of the less heroic aspects of Yugoslavia's resistance to Stalin, and, in the subsequent years, a stream of films, literary works, memoirs and documents completed the picture of Goli otok camp and the circumstances that created it. The author's merit is that he found a way to dramatise the web of ideology and terror within the frame of specific historic events. Now, when the trauma appears to have been mainly overcome, the perverse dialectics whereby ideology yields to terror and then in turn attempts to justify it, as exposed by Jovanović, can be fully grasped by the audience.[15]

III

In the 1980s Jovanović re-examined the link of utopianism and terrorism in his play Military Secret (Vjaška skrivnost, 1983), again referring primarily to the specific Yugoslav problems, but again indicating broader ramifications. This time the action is set in a zoological institute where a group of scientists is attempting to crack the secret of animal speech. The institute is in disarray, the project is in serious trouble and its participants have lost self-confidence and a clear sense of direction. Confu-sion, sloppy work, shortages of equipment, repeated failures and general dissatisfaction at once convey, to the Yugoslav viewer, a familiar picture of Yugoslav society as a whole, as it sinks deeper and deeper throughout the 1980s into crisis. The attitudes of the animals in the institute and of its staff are representative of most political opinions and frustrations that mark Yugoslav society and its various segments: the continuous attraction to the Western market models, *lumpen*-proletariat egalitarianism, petit-bourgeois aspirations, dogmatic authoritarianism, all highlighted by ethnic and regional rivalries. The scientific mission of the institute fades away as it becomes a hospice, a shabby asylum which offers low-quality care for animals in distress.

The arrival of a military officer, sent to keep the institute from falling apart, cannot help the situation: some repressive measures are introduced, stern discipline and isolation from the outer world are imposed, personal choices are curbed, but the goals of the project are rephrased along the way as to acquire an unexpected military significance: not the understanding of the animals, but their training and deployment for military and intelligence-gathering purposes gradually becomes the new goal, a 'low-tech/high-tech' solution for an impoverished developing country in an insecure world.

Despite its fantastic elements, Jovanović's play works primarily as a satire on present Yugoslav ills. The dissonant opinions of the staff and the shrill, often cacophonic disputes among the animals, who incessantly debate, attack each other and promote the advantages and interests of their own species,[16] call to mind the heated atmosphere of Yugoslav public life, the ongoing 'verbal civil war' of too many embattled sides, where too much is being said and too little done to achieve change or at least reach some consensus about prospective change. The scientists cannot understand the animals, but since the animals understand the humans only too well, they can sense when they are being endangered by the staff.

Terror confirms the failure of utopia and marks its transition to dystopia. Animals feud among themselves and live in fear of the staff. Their skirmishes echo perennial confrontations in the world at large. The staff is divided, some members plotting against the others, and all fearful of the officer who takes charge from the old scientist. The elder man is too tired and confused to go on while his replacement shows little understanding of scientific pursuits and the new legal adviser does not help matters much by churning out new by-laws for the institute. There is a pervasive climate of implicit terror, of the government activation of its repressive apparatus to take control over the scientific establishment and made it subservient to its own interests, of the unpredictable assault of free-lance terrorists among the staff. Despite the fantastic setting and the animal protagonists, the atmosphere of terror is made palpable and larger ideological oppositions come alive in the mutual hostility of particular biological species.

Within the walls of the institute, the collective hopes and ambitions of post-war Yugoslav society and its utopian project of 'socialism with a human face', a peculiar brand of decentralised self-management conceived to unify different nations, languages, creeds, and economic priorities, are revealed by the author as being on the verge of collapse. The secret of animal language that Dr Medak has been pursuing in vain is revealed as the ideal of smooth human communication and full understanding among all social groups, between the masses and their leaders. It is postulated as a precondition for full social harmony and expanded individual freedom. As such, the language itself is the ultimate utopian project, now instrumentalised in power games and monopolised by particular interest groups.

But at the point where he has, it seems, developed his situation to its bitterest possibilities, Jovanović shifts from a satiric mode to a grotesque fantasy, and turns from a referential, allegorical discourse (animals made to resemble humans) to a metaphorical one (humans are transformed into animals). When mounting tensions break into open conflict, animal speech becomes the secret whisper of the tortured soul, a yearning for another reality; in a spectacular reversal, Jovanović finds means to re-open the utopian perspective by discarding all utilitarian schemes and manipulative political causes that have blocked it for some time.

In the end, *Military Secret* jumps from the realm of a restrictive necessity to the realm of a desired freedom. It breaks away from the dissatisfaction of the present and turns towards the hopes of the future. The playwright is, at this point, not an advocate of any specific policy nor a propagandist for some pragmatic reform, but an anarchic visionary who transcends the present conflicts and problems with a fresh surge of his own utopian energies. In his capacity as artist, Jovanović is able to mark the future by simply mopping away the 'spiderweb of the Discourse'[17] and the established instruments of terror/terrorism in order to restate the validity of the experiment with a conclusion that remains ambiguous but promising. Such a shift to the irrational could be discarded as escapist, but in its metaphoric vein it befits a play whose fantastic initial assumption (the animals who talk among themselves and understand human speech in its semantic nuances) and built-in theatricality (of human actors playing various animals) can sustain such a highly theatrical ending.[18]

While in *Tumour in the Brain* and *Karamazovs* Jovanović has shown how utopia leads to terror and terrorism and how a ritual pattern of collective interaction and mythical yearning for wholeness collapse in havoc and violence, or in escalating repression, in *Military Secret* allegory is deployed to show the emancipation of utopia and its disengagement from terror. That such a turn-round demands an allegorical frame indicates, I think, the difficulty of sustaining a utopian faith under any circumstances today, most especially because of dominant power systems which tend, as shown in *Military Service*, to co-opt utopias and reduce them to ideologies. We can see terror/terrorism as a catalyst in the conversion of utopia into an ideology or as a key agent in the ideological subversion of utopian aspirations. If *Tumour* displays the immanent dangers of utopian faith, in society as well as in art, the *Karamazovs* uses a historic paradigm to sketch out the pain caused by a fallen utopia, *Military Secret* reminds us what life would be like without utopias, and offers its allegory as a meta-utopian discourse, as antidote against ideological narrow-mindedness and pseudo-utopian gullibility.

IV

The optimistic invocation of utopia that marked the ending of *Military Secret* could not be sustained in the subsequent plays of Dušan Jovanović. In his recent drama, *The Soothsayer* (*Jasnovidka*, 1988) the action is located in the milieu of high Yugoslav politics, where pragmatism is the name of the game, played out under the pressure of a worsening social crisis with high political risks. The Byzantine manoeuvres, alliances made and broken, backstabbings and faked reconciliations show rampant cynicism and both ideology and utopia are discarded as unpleasant liabilities. The former is implicated only in rhetorical utterances that ring hollow; the latter emerges only in a caricatured form as a maddening search for some sudden shift or move that would salvage weakened personal and institutional power. As in the plays of Aristophanes, utopia becomes a naive quest for the miraculous resolution of overwhelming ills, an absurd escapist fantasy.[19]

The Soothsayer has a densely-woven plot that utilises elements and devices from various dramatic genres, including vaudeville, melodrama and farce. It relies on topical allusions, ESP and the motif of a hidden treasure for which embattled factions and characters compete. The comic energy of the play is gradually replaced by a sinister atmosphere in which a broad coalition is formed to gain control over the central character, a person of mystical force and prophetic insight. The extraordinary gift of the woman revealed as the soothsayer is, however, tied to her feeling of love and as the authentic emotions wane in the pervasive insincerity of the group, her rare soothsaying ability is lost. Blindness replaces insight; the invocation of threats and instruments of terror cannot yield any positive results. Opportunistic deals and compromise tactics cannot reinvigorate the politicians or their sidekicks, or endow the society at large with some common sense of purpose. The readiness to apply the methods of terror indicates the degree of social disintegration, the lost sense of community, the compromised institutions on whose ruins politics becomes a Hobbesian war of feuding individuals, each one fighting for his or her own survival. As in some of his previous plays, the author's satiric posture is transformed into an exploration of the uncanny aspects of human existence. The broad societal picture is refocused on the trembling of the tortured individual soul.[20]

V

When individual and collective lives become permeated with politics to the point of saturation, the dramatist's perspective tends to narrow. He is inclined to abandon the arena of great public issues and seek a new series of topics in the sphere of

the intimate individual experience. It should not be so surprising, therefore, that while destruction and disintegration
accelerate in Yugoslav politics, the most recent Jovanović play,
The Wall, the Lake (*Sid, jezero*, 1988) conceives of utopia only as
unachievable conjugal bliss, and presents terror as the marital
guerre de l'attrition, propelled by such a basic human emotion
as jealousy.

A degree of personal and generational self-criticism, going
back to the fallacies of 1968, could be detected in this shift.
The individual is rediscovered as a vast and unique microcosm
worth exploring in the dramatic mode. Jovanović is distancing
himself from the web of utopia, dystopia, and ideology that
has for more than two decades marked the styles of radical
will of his own generation. To a great extent the whole journey
has been an ongoing dispute with the previous generation – of
fathers who have fought and won the war and set the terms
of the modern Yugoslav society, subverted their own utopias
with ideology and packaged ideology as utopia for their children's generation. Sometimes they have even confronted the
utopian aspirations of the young with threats of terror when
they felt it to be necessary to protect their dominant position.[21]

Now in full maturity, Jovanović and his generation are
already being challenged by the following generation that has
little interest in the old battles and little use for the weapons
they were fought with – that is, little use for the whole conceptual apparatus of drama that attempted to grasp and mould
collective consciousness. The opposition is not only formal
and stylistic, and not even limited to a new set of topoi being
introduced. This new generation is in the process of asserting
itself primarily through a different sensitivity and a total
alteration of the world view that is now firmly entrenched in
individuality, rather than in any collectivist project. Jovanović,
who has a rare ability to invent strategic shifts in his career and
achieve creative self-renewal, might be anticipating the development of the members of the new generation while breaking
a path for them and for himself. He is uniquely qualified to
provide this transition since in all the plays discussed here, he
has kept a niche of enigmatic, irrational powers, from which
the vision of the work has been controlled and which endowed
it with an authorial, highly personal quality. In this manner

Jovanović has shown that despite all the rationalist premises of utopianising, despite the attempts to rationalise terrorism in order to dramatise it, drama can only handle this thematic corpus if it contains at least a grain of irrationality. This has been understood by some of the great twentieth-century dramatists of terror and political violence, such as Witkiewicz, Genet and Soyinka.

NOTES

1. For an attempt to systematise these objections, see Raymond Ruyer, *L'Utopie et les utopies* (Paris, 1950), 55-113. Also, George Kateb seeks to refute them in *Utopia and Its Enemies* (New York, 1963).
2. Cf. Gert Ueding, ed., *Literatur ist Utopie* (Frankfurt, 1978); Klaus L. Berghahn and Hans U. Seeber, eds., *Literarische Utopie von Morus zur Gegenwart* (Köningshein, 1983); Peer Alexander and Robert Gill, eds., *Utopias* (London, 1984).
3. Cf. Irwing Howe, ed., *1984 Revisited* (New York, 1983).
4. Described by Norman Cohn in *The Pursuit of Millennium* (1975); rev. ed. (London, 1979).
5. Cf. Vojin Dimitrijević, *Terorizam* (Belgrade, 1982), 149-70.
6. Slobodan Drakulić, Mirjana Oklobdžija and Claudio Venza, *Gradska gerila u Italiji* (Rijeka, 1983), 43-68.
7. Cf. Andrej Inkret, 'Revolucija na odru', *Milo za drago* (Ljubljana, 1978), 14-18.
8. There is an unpublished English translation of the play by Leslie Soule.
9. Cf. R. J. Nelson, *Play Within Play* (New Haven, 1958) and Manfred Schmeling, *Metathéâtre et intertexte, Aspects du théâtre dans le théâtre*, Archives des lettres modernes 204 (Paris, 1982).
10. This led to the decision by some of the prominent Slovenian theatre directors to boycott the Slovenian Popular Theatre (SNG), the central institution of national culture in Slovenia. The boycott lasted for several years.
11. A. Inkret, 'Silovit teater', *op. cit.*, 188-90.
12. Jan Kott, 'Das Ende des unmöglichen Teaters', *Theater Heute*, annual *Theater 1980*, 138 *passim*.
13. This was for the first time publicly acknowledged by Vladimir Dedijer, in *Izgubljena bitka J. V. Staljina* (*Stalin's Lost Battle*) (Sarajevo, 1969), 416-21.
14. See Laszlo Vegél, 'Mogućnost i nemogućnost tragičnog, Borba Dušana Jovanović aza moderne dramske forme', in *Abrahamov nož* (Zagreb, 1987), 53-70.

15. The first intended production (in the National Theatre, Belgrade) was cancelled at dress rehearsal, subsequently never to open. Subsequent professional productions (in Celje, Sarajevo and Zagreb, and later in Skopje) all stirred a great deal of controversy and provoked some officially-inspired rebukes and polemics. Cf. D. Klaić, 'Obsessed with politics', *Scena*, English issue 9 (1986): 7-19.
16. Similarity with Orwell's *Animal Farm* is obvious, but superficial. Cf. Vegél, *op. cit.*, 68-70.
17. Cf. Svetislav Jovanov, 'Povratak Bobija Vatsona, ili: demokratilizam u kavezu', *Rajski trovači* (Belgrade, 1987), 93-107.
18. Especially in the KPGT production of the play, directed by Ljubiša Ristić in Split in the summer 1983, where the puzzle of the future is reclaimed by an innocent six-year-old girl who calls it 'a military secret'.
19. As, for instance, in Aristophanes' *Birds* or *The Women in the Assembly*.
20. *The Soothsayer* still (in March 1989) awaits its first production, to be directed by Ljubiša Ristić, in the National Theater Subotica.
21. 'Comrades, count on your grandsons, they will be your true sons', says Crazy Vava in a monologue towards the end of scene III, 8 of Jovanović's *The Liberation of Skopje* (*Oslobodjenje Skopja* (Zagreb, 1977), 68.

Plays by Dušan Jovanović, discussed above:
Norci (Maribor, 1970).
Igrajte tumor v glavi ali onesnaženje zraka (Maribor, 1972); in Serbocroat in *Oslobodjenje Skopja i druge drame*, trans. N. Toplak (Zagreb, 1981).
Karamazovi (in Serbocroat), trans. R. Njeguš (Belgrade, 1984). English translation by George Mitrevski in *Zagreb Theater Company/KPGT American Tour Program* (Ljubljana and New York, 1982).
Vojaška skrivnost in *Maske* (Ljubljana, 1984). In Serbocroat: *Vojna taina*, trans. G. Janjušević (Belgrade, 1983).
Jasnovidka ali Dan mrtvih (Celovec, 1988). In Serbocroat (trans. G. Janjušević): 'Vidovnica ili Dan mrtvih', *Književne novine* 752 (1988). Also in German as 'Die Hellseherin', trans. K. D. Olof, in *YU Fest '88 National Theater Subotica* (Subotica, 1988).
Zid, jezero (in Serbocroat, trans. J. Osti) in *Scena* 1 (1989).

8

Politics and Terror in the Plays
of Howard Brenton

RICHARD BOON

In late 1971, the British playwright Howard Brenton produced
a play called *A Sky Blue Life: Scenes after Maxim Gorki*.[1] The
piece was about the Russian writer's life and work, and took
the form of biographical scenes -- including real-life meetings
with Tolstoy and Lenin – intercut with dramatised extracts of
Gorki's dramatic and non-dramatic work, extracts in which the
character of Gorki himself played parts. The changing nature
of Gorki's participation from silent observer to active, even
interfering, protagonist, enabled Brenton to raise important
questions about the role and function of the writer in times
of great social crisis (a debate he returned to in his 1984 play
about Shelley, *Bloody Poetry*).[2] In trying to come to terms with
what exactly his responsibilities are, Gorki moves through a
series of roles from writer as poet and moralist (the position
represented the play by Tolstoy), to writer as agent for social
change and propagandist for the revolution, as Lenin would
have him be. For much of the play, Gorki is shown to be
paralysed by the contradictions between the natural flow of
his creative imagination and his intellectual sense of the social
and political function of his work. Often, he is left stranded on
the stage as his characters take on lives of their own.

I begin here because it seems to me that it is impossible
to divorce the politics *in* Brenton's work from the politics *of*
Brenton's work, and because this moment in his career – the
early 1970s – was for him crucial in terms of the need to confront not only questions of *what* one writes, but also questions
of *how* one writes it and for whom.

Brenton's origins as a dramatist lie in the late 1960s. He was

138

part of that great upsurge in avant-garde, oppositional theatrical activity that occurred throughout Europe and America that was itself a manifestation of the wider social and political upheaval which challenged the assumptions and institutions of society, government and culture at their deepest level. His early work, however, was not, in any specific sense, 'political'. Much of it was written out of gut reaction to his own background and education and to what he saw as the irredeemable corruption and decay of society generally and of the theatre in particular. Typically, these early plays were short, designed to tour in a variety of poorly-equipped, non-theatrical venues, and were funny, obscene and violent in character. Many of them were written for the Fringe group Portable Theatre, which he joined in 1969. The philosophy of Portable Theatre, insofar as it had one, was anti-theatrical, anti-cultural and anti-humanistic, designed to provoke, antagonise and confront its audiences. Brenton's 1970 play, *Christie in Love*,[3] was typical. Its hero was the mass sex-murderer Reginald Christie, whose life and crimes were presented sympathetically in the context of a nihilistic, black satire that viciously lampooned all forms of authority and conventional standards of justice and decency, arguing that these were no more than inadequate and hypocritical responses from a public whose real interest lay in a salacious voyeurism. Christie constitutes the clearest expression of Brenton's intentions in this early work, where many of his heroes are obsessive, violent, vengeful figures who nonetheless possess a kind of straightforward integrity that those about them lack. These are the figures who were to develop into the terrorist-heroes of later work, but at this stage the political outlook of the work, such as it is, is unformed and instinctive, and lacks any relation to a larger, systematised, progressive school of thought.

What began to develop Brenton's political sense was a growing awareness of events in France in 1968. He visited Paris in 1969, and, in common with a whole generation of young British playwrights (including David Hare, Trevor Griffiths and David Edgar), was politically energised by what he saw there. It should be noted that what was important here was less a complete commitment to the ideals of the alternative culture than shock and revulsion at the brutality with which the state crushed those ideals and those who believed in them, and it is this sense of outrage that informs the plays Brenton wrote out of the experience. What also informed them was the influence of one important strand of thinking that emerged from the radical redefinition of political thought on the left that has been the major legacy of the May, 1968 'événements': Situationism.

This essay is not the occasion for a detailed examination of what is a complex political theory, but some limited account of it may be useful if its importance to Brenton is to be understood. Broadly speaking, the Situationists offered a reassessment of the traditional Marxist view of the basic relationship between the individual and his society. The need to change society remained, of course, paramount, but conventional political struggle – not only parliamentary democracy, industrial relations and so on, but Marxist revolution itself – was rejected as no more than the deployment of tactics within an existing system that would remain fundamentally unchanged. That system was defined as the 'society of the spectacle'. The Situationist analysis argued that the mainspring of capitalist repression had ceased to be located at the point of production – on the factory floor – and had transferred to a point of consumption: the consumption of bourgeois ideology as transmitted through culture generally and the mass media in particular. The relationship between the individual and society was thus analogous to that between the spectator and the events on a screen: both were passive consumers of a two-dimensional charade. It was by shattering the hegemony of the received images that individuals had of society that the ground-work of revolutionary change could be established; smashing the screen of *public* life would expose the realities of *private* and *daily* life beneath.[4]

It is impossible to identify a particular moment when Situationism began to influence Brenton's thinking. Arguably Situationist ideas are present in embryonic form in the public–private dichotomies of plays like *Christie*; but as I have suggested, those plays were as much reflections of personal 'anti-culturalism' as of any wider political view. Moreover, what Brenton took from the Situationists was less a brand-new philosophy than a framework of systematic thought which both confirmed his own views and provided a context for their further development. Brenton's assimilation of Situationist ideas was a slow process, based on the need to test and explore them practically through his writing for the stage, and not coming to full fruition until his first full-scale play, *Magnificence*, in 1973. But Situationist thought does emerge as a visible influence in two pieces written for Portable Theatre in 1970 and 1972: 'Fruit' a short touring play, and 'Skin Flicker', a forty-minute film.[5]

'Fruit' is a wild, violent, often obscene piece, written as a response to the 1970 General Election in Britain which saw the installation of a right-wing government under Edward Heath. As such, it is the first of Brenton's plays to make the political world overtly its subject, and the first to be written as a direct response to contemporary events. Its central character is Paul, a victim of the thalidomide tragedy, who has risen to a position of power as 'Osteopath to the Great'. He uses his privileged position to blackmail the new Prime Minister, who is a closet homosexual. His attempt fails, however, and he is forced to go on the run, eventually meeting an old Leninist Trade Unionist who berates him for his lack of political analysis and ends by showing him – and the audience – how to make *and use* a petrol-bomb. The bomb is thrown against the back wall of the theatre. *'God knows'*, read Brenton's stage-directions,*'how we are going to get away with that'*.

Paul is first in the line of Brenton's hero-terrorists. Where his dramatic predecessors take their revenge only on immediate authority-figures – parents, teachers, policemen – Paul's targets are the leading figures of public life: politicians, bishops, media-men. His all-consuming passion for personal revenge is centred on what he perceives to be the conspiracy of public institutions: the drug company, which made him a monster, the politicians who capitalised on the scandal, the media and the fashionable magazines which exploited his 'human interest' story. It is the Prime Minister's role as the figurehead of public life *generally* that makes him the target of blackmail, as Paul threatens to smash that public role by revealing the private reality of the Prime Minister's homosexuality. The point is an important one, because it helps define the limited sense in which 'Fruit' is a political play. The

Situationists themselves were concerned less with the prom-
ulgation of specific political courses of action than with the
need to challenge and disrupt the wider cultural stranglehold
society maintained on its members. Paul's attack on the Prime
Minister is not in any particular or partisan sense a political
action: it is a matter of personal revenge, a glorified version
of events at the beginning of the play when, infuriated by the
bland posturings of politicians on television, he kicks in the
screen of his TV set. And he fails precisely because he under-
estimates the power of 'the spectacle': the Prime Minister is
unmoved by his threats because he is confident his public
image is powerful enough to overcome any revelation about
his private life. Paul's defeat is compounded by the old Trade
Unionist, whose alternative – classic Marxist-Leninist revolution – is presented as archaic and redundant. For him, using
petrol bombs is a handy stop-gap measure: for Brenton in
1970, it is the only 'political' and 'realistic' line of attack: '[a]
really great outburst of nihilism like "Fruit" . . . is one of the
most beautiful and positive things you can see on a stage', he
wrote.[6]

Thematically, 'Skin Flicker' treads similar ground to 'Fruit',
but its conclusions are quite different. Brenton's script is pref-
aced by his own synopsis of the plot:

> A teacher, a nurse and a garrulous layabout kidnap a pub-
> lic man somewhere in England. They employ a camera-
> man, a maker of blue films, to record what happens. The
> story ends with the defection of the cameraman, the mur-
> der of the public man, and the suicide of the kidnappers.
> At a later date the material shot for the film is edited by
> government officials for 'training' purposes, to instruct
> public employees in the *mores* of extremist groups.[7]

Here the stress is on waste and futility. Actions genuine
in impulse and justified in their anger are fatally undermined by a lack of proper understanding of the nature of
the enemy, and of the need to organise action from within
a wide theoretical framework. Without that framework, the
kidnappers' actions are reduced to the level of 'politics as
psycho-drama',[8] and worse: their film is a positive help to
their enemies. 'Skin Flicker' is presented in a wider historical
and political context than 'Fruit': its story was inspired by a

real-life incident, the Laporte kidnapping in Canada in 1970, and deals by implication with the contemporary growth of terrorist groups such as the Angry Brigade It also differs from 'Fruit' crucially, in one further respect: it deals less with a single hero than with a group of figures of comparable importance. As such, it enabled Brenton to create the dramatic space for debate, for argument to take place, ideas to be examined and decisions made openly. This move towards a more dialectical style of writing is reflected in the film's structure, indeed in the fact that the material was made as a film at all. It is not surprising that, given the basic tenets of Situationism, Brenton should take the opportunity to write for the screen. The political analysis of 'the society of the spectacle', as has been seen, naturally borrows the language of film and television to express itself; 'Skin Flicker' simply makes use of that communality of language and ideas. The terrorists' use of a pornographer to record their actions not only underlines the obscenity of their violence, but also, in a wider sense, comments on the reaction of an audience more interested in the spectacle of that violence than in the political issues raised, a point emphasised further by the title. Moreover, the very structure of the film dramatises the difficulties and dangers of how a piece of drama is received and can be used. The incompetent actions of the young terrorists become a 'snuff movie', which in turn is appropriated by the state to train its own counter-terrorist operatives. This structure of a film-within-a-film-within-a-film, as one critic puts it, 'raises quite consciously questions about the role of a radical drama set in a non-radical theatrical context which are crucial . . .'.[9]

These are questions which come to dominate Brenton's thinking generally in the early 1970s. Even as 'Skin Flicker' was being made, Brenton was beginning to move from the fringes of theatrical activity to the mainstream, to try to get his voice heard on the large, established public stages. The move was precipitated by his perception that the Fringe was becoming an artistic cul-de-sac, its audiences as particular and unrepresentative of society in general as their West End counterparts. The 'artistic terrorism' of the Portable work appealed less to the spectator's political sense than to an increasingly sophisticated appreciation of the pieces as experiments in *style*. Like many of the characters in their plays, the Portable writers found themselves, to borrow Alain Touraine's phrase, caught 'in an encounter between a revolutionary movement and a non-revolutionary situation'.[10]

Brenton did not, however, simply ditch the Fringe. Although since 1973 the majority of his work has been produced in the established theatre, he has not only continued to write for the alternative theatre circuit, but has also consistently sought to bring into the mainstream the language and the political preoccupations of the Fringe. The first play to attempt to do this was *Magnificence* (a piece which has a subtext precisely about the difficulties its writer faces in getting his work accepted by a big public theatre: in the first scene, it takes the characters some considerable time to get on stage at all).

The play was produced in London's Royal Court Theatre, a theatre with a long tradition of encouraging new writing and the obvious place for a writer like Brenton to turn to. In *Magnificence* Brenton is engaged fully for the first time with contemporary political issues, although 'conventional left politics' are left 'completely out of account'. Rather, it 'was written to try to resolve the author's confusions about the nature of revolutionary action';[11] as such, its concerns are with the aftermath of 1968, with smashed idealism, the failure of the alternative culture and the emergence of the terrorist. It was inspired in part by the attack of the Angry Brigade on the house of Robert Carr, Government Minister for Employment, in 1971. Houses, in fact, become a central image in the play. A derelict house is taken over by a group of young people, squatters making a political statement about the injustice of government housing policy. As a group they are energetic and idealistic, but from the start they are also shown to be incompetent, divided and inward-looking: they spray slogans and hang banners, but on inside walls. The play's crisis comes when they are evicted. Their resistance is dealt with brutally, and one of them, a pregnant girl, rather symbolically loses her baby when kicked in the stomach by a bailiff. Her lover, Jed, goes to gaol for two years, and emerges bent on revenge.

What is significant about *Magnificence* is that although it is

'about' 1968, it was written five years later, and is more concerned with the aftermath of the 'événements' than with their
historical moment. Its key question is what happens next. By
the middle of the play the group of squatters has dispersed;
some have simply drifted away and one, at least, has become
a drug-raddled parody of his early idealistic self. But Jed's
political commitment has hardened. He is the culmination of
Brenton's line of hero-terrorists (similar figures recur in later
work, but, as shall be seen, are treated rather differently). His
closest ancestor is Paul in 'Fruit', but where Paul's passion for
revenge is purely personal and largely instinctive, Jed's is part
of a wider and more clearly understood political struggle. He
has read his Marx and Lenin, and initially accepts the case for
carefully planned and engineered mass revolution. But his
need for vengeance, born of his personal tragedy, leads him
down the path of the bomber, his goal the Situationists 'magnificent' gesture of defilement of the bland face of public life.
His chosen target is the government minister of housing, but
Jed picks him as much for his symbolic value as for any actual
connection with the original political aims of the squat. The
Minister has already been identified in the play as representative of the new-style, media politician, prepackaged for public
consumption like 'Bloody breakfast cereal'. Personally he is
charming and urbane, if corrupt, but his civilised humanism is
rejected by Jed as simply part of the process of obfuscation by
which the English 'society of the spectacle' maintains its grip.
The manner of the attempted assassination confirms where
Jed's preoccupations – or obsessions – lie: his chosen weapon
is neither the rifle of the cool professional political assassin,
nor the axe of the psychopath: it is a bomb, a *string of gelignite . . . arranged round a sack*, and tied around the politician's
head. Its function is not simply to kill the individual, but to
destroy his image – the two-dimensional, bland image that
smiles from the TV and thereby bring about a rupture in the
screen that represents a deeply-fraudulent myth of public life.
The revenger's disgust and revulsion toward his victim, and
the theoretical framework of Situationism, combine to make
Jed's voice the most powerful in the play. And yet even as
Brenton, for the first time, fully finds that voice, he questions
the validity of what is being said.

Events themselves under-cut the 'heroism' of Jed's action. The sense of absurd incompetence which dogs the squatters in scene one resurfaces in the final scene to mock the 'purity' of his revenge: not only does his bomb initially fail to explode, but his victim has been demoted, and is no longer responsible for government housing policy. (Similarly, the Angry Brigade's attack on Robert Carr was made futile by the fact that he was away on holiday, and his home was empty.) Even as a symbol, Jed's Minister proves disarmingly human rather than reassuringly two-dimensional. In this way, Jed finds that the 'magnificence' of his gesture is itself defiled, and the eventual accidental explosion of the bomb, killing both the Minister *and* Jed, becomes no more than a moment of grotesque and horrific comedy. For Brenton, this is now 'the inevitable consequence of that kind of action . . . undisciplined, anarchic bombing versus a collapsing middle class. The streets run with blood and politically there's no one to pick up the pieces.'[12] This stands in stark contrast to his position at the end of 'Fruit', where nothing contradicts the argument of the bomber. Indeed, the old syndicalist's justification for bombing – 'On the other hand, while we're waiting for the Thames to run red, and all that, we can get on' – is precisely why Jed rejects the Leninist line. *Magnificence* pushes the argument further: the bomber's action is shown to be futile, his political position untenable.

The main agent for questioning the usefulness of Jed's action is his friend Cliff. It is he who speaks Jed's epitaph, lamenting the waste of his life. But neither the righteousness of Jed's anger, nor the morality of political violence is questioned. It is Jed's *tactics* that Cliff rejects, tactics that have become nothing more than 'some fucking stupid gesture', an issue of personal revenge rather than of political struggle. The crucial weakness in Jed's position is his unrealistic romanticism. The prison cell which nurtured his terrorism is as inward-looking and remote from daily reality as the squatters' room had been. The rejection of Jed's politics of the 'magnificent gesture' in favour of the more pragmatic tactics of continuing argument and organisation represented by Cliff is not an easy step for Brenton. As one critic suggests, what happens in *Magnificence* is 'a hard-won rediscovery of the politics rejected by his early work'.[13] Moreover, Cliff's alternative

('corny work') is, at this stage in the author's career, offered
only as a general approach: it is not until later – notably' in
The Churchill Play – that Brenton is able to articulate more fully
a brand of political activism which can genuinely match the
ferocious anger of the bomber.

This is the crucial weakness of *Magnificence*. Despite Brenton's rejection of Jed *politically*, *theatrically* the play is his.
Cliff, potentially Jed's most powerful critic, is simply too
silent, and Jed remains unequivocally the hero of the piece.
But he's a hero who is 'wrong'. As Brenton points out, 'part
of the humanist structure of plays, is the assumption that the
person with whom the audience spends the most time, and
with whom the playwright spends most time, is right'.[14] But
the audience's ability to judge Jed's wrongness is compromised by a too-silent Cliff, and the play becomes *simply* Jed's
tragedy, its 'humanist structure' intact.

The theatrical ramifications of moving from small Fringe
spaces to larger public ones are enormous, affecting every
aspect of play-making. Inevitably, perhaps, *Magnificence* only
partially succeeds in making the transition: it remains a
hybrid play, half Fringe, half new, expanded, epic theatre.
It does however, break important new ground in one vital
respect: like 'Skin Flicker', it attempts to supplant the individual hero with a group of figures. To a degree, Brenton's
motives are again born of doubts regarding the 'humanist
hero'. To internalise a debate about political issues within
the mind of a single figure is to run the risk of psychologising
that debate, of making issues of politics, issues of character.
That he should choose to 'externalise' the dialectics, to make
the debate overt by staging it among a number of individual
characters, indicates what kind of relationship with the audience Brenton is intent on. Groups of figures of different attitudes, background and experience give him the opportunity to
explore a writing-style that lends itself readily to argument and
counter-argument, and, equally important, that allows him to
ground that argument in a social reality which an audience
can verify and authenticate from its own experience. The first
scene of *Magnificence* is marked by an increased variety, depth
and sophistication of characterisation and interaction between
characters, where individual and social processes are shown to

be inseparable from political processes. As I have argued, the play does not sustain this: Jed escapes the group theatrically and takes the play with him. But this is the last time Brenton allows it to happen. Comparable figures in later work – Jimmy in *The Churchill Play*, Ken in *Weapons of Happiness* – remain within the groups they are part of, dramatically contained. The emphasis shifts from the portrayal of the career of a lone revenger to the careful mapping of the sociopolitical dynamics of groups, synthesising political message and social reality.

In artistic terms, Brenton sees this is a crucial element in the creation of a new British epic theatre of political and social argument. Politically, it marks his final rejection of individual acts of terrorism as viable courses of action. But this is not to say at the debate does not continue in later work. His adaptation of Büchner's *Danton's Death* for the National Theatre in 1982 indicates his continuing preoccupation with the conflicting claims of a passionate, pure, anarchic idealism on the one hand and a cool, ruthless, disciplined pragmatism on the other.[15] But the terrorists who do recur in later plays are of a different kind from their ancestors. The 1981 play *Thirteenth Night* describes a left-wing coup in Britain which rapidly slides into Stalinist dictatorship before itself being toppled by a second, more radical coup, whose representatives are three mysterious women terrorists.[16] Their dramatic function, however, is quite different from earlier manifestations: no real indication is given of who or what they represent, what their specific aims are, or how they are organised. They are almost visitors from another world, one more just and free, and as such they throw into relief the failings of the new government. In *The Romans in Britain* (1980), a play which tackles the subject of the British presence in Ireland by placing it in the wider context of an analysis of the nature of imperialism generally, the IRA terrorists shown are accounted for as inevitable functions of that imperialism. Their actions are neither condemned nor condoned: they are simply the logical consequence of the injustice of invasion and colonisation.[17]

In all these plays, the terrorists' case is part of a wider debate, one element in a complex social, political and historical argument. Where in the early work history itself is disregarded or attacked as an appropriation of 'the society of the spectacle', the later plays insist on the need to confront and learn from the past. A piece like *The Churchill Play* still debunks official versions of history by questioning attitudes to dead great men in a typical Situationist manner, but it also warns that debunking is not enough. In *Weapons of Happiness*, a group of squatters not unlike those in *Magnificence* is eventually set on a realistic course of political action by listening to the experiences of an old Czech refugee, a victim of the Stalinist purges of the 1950s who cannot quite kill off his belief in communism. Even in *Thirteenth Night*, a play Brenton wrote out of a belief that the British left needed to face the bloodstained history of communism, the figure who over the course of the play effectively becomes Stalin is given, on the moment of his death, a speech challenging the audience to face the reality that any revolution must inevitably spill the blood of its enemies if it is genuinely to succeed. And, most obviously, *Romans* deals centrally with the whole process of how history is made and used. In attacking, in that play, some of the most sacred mythologies within British historiography, Brenton brought to the very heart of official culture – the National Theatre – the kind of thinking more usually confined to the margins or the underbelly of public life.

Finally, there remains the continuing debate about the political strategy of trying to penetrate mainstream official culture with radical oppositional argument. For some, Brenton has sold out; for others, he remains the 'wolf within the gates' of the established theatre. I make only the following point. To refuse to enter into argument on the public stage, however great the risks of appropriation might be, is effectively to surrender the high ground to 'the enemy'. Brenton's own belief is that interventionist work can dislocate and disrupt the flow of oppressive official culture, planting within it new images, ideas and questions. His metaphor is of a prisoner in a cell, knocking on the pipes to communicate with his fellow prisoners. It is not altogether a satisfactory idea, nor a particularly comforting one. But I return to the figure of Gorki in *A Sky Blue Life*. In that play's last scene, the writer, again playing a role in one of his own stories, pretends to be a medical student in order to force his help on a woman giving birth. She resists his solicitations, but he nonetheless

succeeds in delivering the child – a fine, healthy one. Finally,
he has accepted his responsibilities. To one side of the stage,
Lenin stands laughing.

NOTES

1. Howard Brenton, *A Sky Blue Life: Scenes after Maxim Gorki*,
   in *Three Plays*, ed. and with an introduction by John Bull
   (Sheffield: Sheffield Academic Press, 1989).
2. Howard Brenton, *Bloody Poetry* (London: Methuen, 1985).
3. Howard Brenton, *Christie in Love*, in *Plays: One* (London:
   Methuen, 1986). This volume also contains *Magnificence*,
   The Churchill Play, *Weapons of Happiness*, *Epsom Downs* and
   Sore Throats.
4. The key Situationist text is Guy Debord, *La Société du
   Spectacle*; a good translation is that produced in Detroit
   by the Black and Red Printing Cooperative, 1970.
5. Neither 'Fruit" nor 'Skin Flicker' is published. I am grateful
   to Howard Brenton for allowing me access to typescripts.
6. Quoted in Peter Ansorge, 'Underground Explorations No.
   1: Portable Playwrights', *Plays and Players* 19, no. 5 (February 1972): 18.
7. Taken from Brenton's typescript.
8. E. P. Thompson, quoted by Brenton in his Preface to
   Plays: One.
9. John Bull, *New British Political Dramatists* (London: Macmillan, 1984), 25.
10. Quoted by Bull, *op. cit.*, 4.
11. Brenton, Preface to *Plays: One*.
12. Brenton, interview with Ronald Hayman, *New Review* 3,
    no. 29 (1976): 57.
13. Bull, *op. cit.*, 50.
14. Brenton, quoted in Catherine Itzin and Simon Trussler,
    'Petrol Bombs Through the Proscenium Arch', *Theatre
    Quarterly* 5, no. 17 (1975): 18.
15. Georg Büchner, *Danton's Death*, adapted by Howard Bren-
    ton from a translation by Jane Fry (London: Methuen,
    1982).
16. Howard Brenton, *Thirteenth Night. A dream play* (London:
    Methuen, 1981).
17. Howard Brenton, *The Romans in Britain* (London: Meth-
    uen, 1980).

9

Images of Terrorism in Contemporary British Drama: Unlocking the World

DAVID IAN RABEY

Dedicated to Ian Cooper

In the early 1980s I wrote a study of modern British and Irish drama which intended to pay tribute to an emergent tradition of radical drama and its subversive potential. In the intervening years, history and experience have taught me that this drama was neither radical nor subversive enough. This essay partially represents a self-conscious reassessment of some dramatists and of the critical standpoint from which I established my credentials.

I shall start, however, not with drama but with fiction. William Burroughs' recent novel *The Place of Dead Roads* (1986) posits the existence of the Johnson Family, an underground network dedicated to acts of disruption. They claim to represent 'Potential America'. Planet Earth is defined as a penal colony mapped out by arch-conservatives. Space represents an escape from a predictable control-oriented universe, into a sphere of liberation as opposed to the current world of filmic and prescriptive prerecordings used as models for human thought and action. The Johnson family's most effective tactic in the 'soul warfare' of disrupting definitions and in the fight against 'the monumental fraud of planet earth' is their willingness to swap locations on an interpersonal basis as a result of the spatial elusiveness of their city, and their capacity to adapt. An apparent mass suicide at their fort cloaks the fact that the outlaws have merely 'disbanded and scattered'; their principle agents keep turning up from Siberia to Timbuktu. The protagonist Johnson, Kim Carsons, is one of ten clones

151

from 'Kim Carsons the Founder' in contact with 'approximate replicas of himself and other clone families'.

Burroughs' novel is notable for its visualisation of the sub-versive cell *from the inside*. Thomas Pynchon's novel *The Crying of Lot 49* (1966) derives imaginative energy from its own dawning impression of an underground Potential America, the Trystero Conspiracy. But the narrative point of view is that of Oedipa Maas, a researcher making deductions from the standpoint of contemporary 1960s society at large. The alternative offers a titillatory *frisson* of possibilities, but none of them are ever fully countenanced, let alone embraced. The individual is isolated, foregrounded against the network, defined in separation from it, and, possibly, in opposition to it.

Formally, images of terrorism in British drama are general-ly closer to Pynchon's viewpoint than to Burroughs'. Howard Brenton's *Magnificence* (1973) dissipates its energy in a first half geared to providing a humanist apologia for the motivation of its protagonist, Jed, who is subsequently sundered even from his erstwhile fellow-squatters by his prison sentence and his guerilla resolve. Jed is inspired to emulate the disruption of consumerist spectacle and vicarious living that he had once witnessed in a cinema when a drunk threw a bottle through a film screen showing *The Carpetbaggers* (and, more precisely, through Carole Baker's left breast). Jed's own plan for 'an entertainment for the oppressed' involves an attack on a Con-servative MP nicknamed Alice, noted even by his peers as a particularly 'silky', 'peculiarly English form of fascist', whose 'honeyed words' on television have a 'silicone effect. Coating the tube with a silvery slime'.[1] Jed's impulse to staunch the coagulating flow of bland harmonisation resembles the attack of the Johnsons on the imagery of prerecorded film. But Jed can offer no counter-imagery of network, purpose or Other World. He perceives his disjunction from the theoretical dicta of Lenin, and denounces the posturings of his former com-rades, whose revolt has degenerated into style. Will, a fellow-squatter and revolutionary, admits that his Che Guevara T-shirt might equally bear the image of Marilyn Monroe, Mickey Mouse, the Apollo moon landing, the Stars and Stripes, or the Hammer and Sickle. The shirt makes him a walking version of a cinema screen, an inanimate recipient of projection.

On confronting Alice, Jed fastens onto the offensive function of the Tory Member of Parliament, his glutinous media-
tion couched in disarming and sickly-sentimental imagery:
'That wrinkled stuff with the picture of English Life in its
pink, rotten meat. In your head. And the nasty tubes to your
eyes that drip Englishness over everything you see. That cool,
glycerine humanity of your tears that smarms our ANGER.
. . . The goo, the sticky mess of your English humanity that
gums up our ears to your lies, our eyes to your crimes'.[2] But
even Alice can absorb and parrot Jed's jargon, deducing that
he intends a 'disruption. A spectacle against the spectacle. A
firework in the face of the ruling class'. Jed's frustration at the
bankruptcy of terminology and the weaponry of resistance
makes him inadvertently detonate some gelignite, killing both
Alice and himself. His ex-comrade Cliff moralises over their
corpses, cementing Jed verbally into the grave with his neat
headstone judgement: 'waste of anger'. The resulting play
is an 'entertainment for the oppressed' in a very debilitating
sense. It is mainly significant for its symptomatic depiction
of an English lack of imaginative persistence, that is to say,
a lack of persistence in the face of the dominant imagery of
respectability. Jed's isolation and foregrounding against his
world gives *Magnificence* the form of the traditional drama on
the English commercial stage, that of private readjustment. As
John O'Brien has noted, the problem with the drama of private
readjustment is that 'the contexts of behaviour remain external
to the protagonist and are ultimately unchangeable'.[3]

Trevor Griffiths' play *Real Dreams* (1987), adapted from
Jeremy Pikser's story *'Revolution in Cleveland'*, draws on an
American source and setting but is essentially a further English drama of private readjustment still depicting, fourteen
years later, the wilful ghettoisation of representatives of the
Left in squats. Griffiths' young white radicals of 1969 are in a
position of shame when receiving a directive from the neigh-
bourhood leader of SPIC (Spanish People In Cleveland). The
leader snorts: 'You gotta talk about it? You bin talkin' for
weeks, man. 'S all you people ever do'.[4] The pivotal character
is Sandler, self-consciously off-balance and articulate, whose
characteristic reflectiveness earns him a rebuff from a fellow
member of the collective: 'Just shut the fuck *up*, Sandler.

This's a fuckin' *action*, man.'[5] Sandler himself speaks of the resistance of essential inclinations, of history as 'unlikely people doing the things they're afraid to do and maybe don't want to do in the first place',[6] without specifying who is to be considered unlikely and why. As in other Griffiths plays, (hetero-) sexual relationships represent an ensnaring distraction from political activism. Sandler recognises his own demand for control over his ex-lover, while a couple in the group separate because of the 'objective correctness' of freeing one member as a woman for the revolution. As the group leader Jack observes that definitions are scrambled when the groups attracts hostility from the SPICs, 'We're protecting our goddam womenfolk. From the savages. Only what we're *supposed* to be doin' is *joinin'* the savages'.[7] Sexuality is identified as carrying white, bourgeois attitudes of possessiveness which define the group essentially as 'cowboys' unable to merge with the primal liberation and sexual potency of the 'Indians'. Later in the play, Sandler helps Jack through tremors of doubt and pays tribute to the persistence of 'real dreams' even as he records his personal lapse into exhaustion and marathon television viewing. The members of the collective are essentially – and they feel, unnecessarily – secluded. Sandler's role as repository for audience sympathy and the focus of their perspective is analogous to watching Pynchon's Oedipa Maas hoping to be recruited by the Trystero while remaining inwardly conscious of its ultimate impossibility.

Edward Bond's *The Worlds* (1979) dramatises the relationship between a businessman, Trench, and a group of activists who kidnap him. A government representative claims that 'Civilisation is built on the finding of substitutes for violence in the conduct of human affairs'.[8] The activists, however, would view this as another deliberately loaded definition. One of them argues: 'the public means of explanation – press, television, theatres, courts, schools, universities – almost everywhere ideas are formed or information is collected is owned in one way or another by people like you' – meaning Trench. He continues, 'Even our language is owned by you. We have to learn a different language. Even our morals. We have to be different people.'[9] Terry, one of Trench's employees on strike, extends this charge to the legal system while even

Trench himself, betrayed by his business peers, is alienated by conventional moral language. He tells them that 'terrorists stand things on their head. Turn values upside down. But the police go after them! You do it and vote yourself a rise!'[10] Yet the activists die in a shoot-out with the police, and the strikers feel bound to condemn them, all except Terry who views both incident and response as confirmation of a socially-controlled language. He contemptuously dismisses the press release of the strikers and stands the moral condemnation of terror on its head:

'Militants condemn terror.' So everyone's still got their right label. We can go home happy. What good's that? . . . The poor are starving. The rich are getting ready to blow [the world] up. Terrorists threaten with guns. We do it with bombs. . . . We don't understand what we are or what we do. That's more dangerous than bombs. We're all terrorists. Everyone of us. We live by terror. . . .

How long can we go on like this? Yet we sit here as if we had all the time in the world. All of us: we sit.

When you ask me to condemn terror I shall say: no. *You* have no right to ask. You are a terrorist.[11]

The events of *The Worlds* have propelled Terry to these dislocating deductions but entrenched others in their moral positions, so that the activists' initiative, like Jed's in *Magnificence*, is annexed by the dominant definitions to bolster their own polarisations. They have proved insufficiently unpredictable as a rupturing of prerecorded responses, except for passing their knowledge on to Terry, who is further isolated by possessing it. Bond depicts the subversive cell as terminally besieged, even eroded, in its effect in terms of potential firepower. The activists Michael, Lisa and Ann may be interchangeable in team terms but are facelessly anonymous with little purchase on the imagination. Their speeches to Trench tend to substitute a worker-based authoritarian ideology for a management one. Their terminology is control-oriented rather than liberationist, while their mission is elitist and intellectual – 'Only the working class can develop our wasting humanity and make society rational' – compared to the mischievous physicality of Burroughs' Johnson family.

Like Cordelia in Bond's *Lear*, Bond's activists wish to adopt existing imagery rather than explode out of it.

Appeals to intellectualism are significantly by-passed in Ron Hutchinson's *Rat in the Skull* (1984), which probably accounts for the difficulties university students experience when grappling with it. In my teaching experience, they are dismayed by the lack of an entry point via ideas. Instead, Roche the Republican and Nelson, the RUC officer, have their own senses of purpose and imagery which mock P. C. Naylor's equivalent tribal status as a 'Tottenham suppporter'. Roche signs a statement of confession, following an urge bred out of 'A thousand Sundays muttering into the God Box', briefly relieved at the certainty of definition which even guilt seductively promises: 'there's something fine and grand and flying high about saying, yes, you've got your man, you're on the ball all right, this is Michael Patrick de Valera Demon Bomber Roche bang to rights.'[12] Nelson wryly speaks of his own status as 'half of Anglo-Irish, Irish-Scots. Anglo-Scots, Irish-Brit, but never just the one, and certain fact, one thing for sure in the entire bloody boiling – now way straight Irish on the rocks.'[13] Yet he links himself to Roche in experience through the one ceremony they have in common, that of following coffins down the street. For all his determination to get inside Roche, however, and for his parodying of 'old, old stories' of glorious lineage, he riles the Republican into loss of control by performing his own version of 'sheer blind sectarian hate'. At the same time as their respective versions of history clash, Nelson can claim they share a sense of purpose through their implacable opposition to the other's kind. '*We* belonged – And we felt what we did for the love of it – *for* – not against, not just against'.[14] Several times, Nelson's movements echo the iconic '*gesture of release and triumph*' which established the image of the Red Hand in Ulster, and both characters share a sense not only of nationalist interest, but also of membership in a religious elect.

Roche and Nelson do not present anyone with intellectual or theoretical conclusions. Isolated in the London police station, they discover *ways of speaking* – lines of images, rhetoric and elected purpose which drown doubt, the 'rat in the skull', and place them beyond the range of conciliation by the uncomprehending language of the English police, which finds no such imaginative richness nor totality of appeal. Nelson finds release from his uncertain sense of nationality and his marital break-up, into the grim certainty of ancestral iconography, where the simple fact of being is inescapable sin. 'The crime is breathing. Don't bring your revolutionary justice, or your religious squawkings into it. . . . I owe those dead men in my dad's Parade that much, at least.'[15] Nelson and Roche only begin to triumph imaginatively when their hatred is liberated by being in brief but common exile in London.

Howard Barker's protagonists tend to be more successful in their subverting and hijacking of official imagery, their defacing of dominant iconography – but only, that is, after the writing of *Credentials of a Sympathiser* (1979). This play depicts, among other things, the coercive strategy of English definition as it is expertly wielded by Gildersleeve, the immaculate government negotiator. His adversary, the Irish Republican leader, Tully, bridles at the description 'terrorist'. 'That is their word', he declares. 'They are the terrorists.' He prefers to claim he is only carrying out 'military operations'. He spends time, accordingly, fighting for free space from official definitions: 'I only ask you to recognise we are soldiers, and treat us accordingly.'[16] The Republicans diffuse their self-control and expend their energy on a duel of words in which they are outmatched. In a flourish of professed concession to his adversaries, Gildersleeve replaces his term 'convicted criminal' with the nonsense word 'buzz', after having perceived Tully's growing impatience with the slow process of negotiation. This ridiculous cipher keeps negotiations ludicrously abstract, further away from the 'people being beatens in their gaols' of which Tully is ever mindful. Gildersleeve levers Tully away from the support of his fellows by demanding the retraction of a rhetorical figure of speech which imputes Nazi methods and sympathies to him. Tully's men are adamantly unmoved. prompting the Republican leader to fantasise his assassination by their hand for being a reactionary. As an exercise in locating potential compromisers in Republican ranks, Gildersleeve's gamesmanship is triumphant. The Republicans are splintered and the formal procedures of negotiation serve the purposes only of the government representatives. It is no wonder, then, that Hacker, who caters for the negotiations, gleefully proclaims 'Terrorists may come and terrorists may go, but conferences will last forever.'[13]

If we turn to Barker's later writings we can note a substantial change of direction. The protagonist of the dramatic monologue *Gary the Thief* (1987) is a criminal who actively exults in negative disassociation. He sees himself as the incarnation of the people's nightmares. Having been merely a negative reflection of the accepted image of society, he decides to be more inventive. In Burroughs' terms, instead of inverting a prerecording, he will embody *a priori* selfhood, and 'mirror the pains / Of a life of opportunity' for the inspiration of others. This is to be done through his new persona of *Gary Upright*. He attempts to rouse passers-by to self-forgiveness and self-liberation even as they muffle such impulses. Gary Upright insists on the power of upheaval in the omnipresent chance of disarray. 'You pile up sentences and like the lag / Dread to be cast out the little door / A free woman'. Gary Upright insists on the power of upheaval in the omnipresent chance of 'disarray': 'I tell the possible / Which must have effects.' These effects extend to the continuance of life through self-reinvention, 'being unkinder', and refusing to accept limitations with which others try to encumber him as a substitute for lived experience. Whereas Gary the Thief's denial was a revelry in the mischief of transgression, Gary Upright persists in life with reference to nothing but himself, in the hope that he will inspire others to do the same, but without imposing an ideology on them. Their discoveries must be their own. In this way, Gary Upright is the ultimate disruption of the control-oriented universe.

In his role and project as the liberator of perception, Gary Upright has affinities with two other Barker renegades, Sordido in in the adaptation of Middleton's *Women Beware Women* (1986) and Starhemberg in *The Europeans* (1987), both of whom hijack iconography at the level of physicality – Sordido by raping Bianca, Starhenberg by sundering Concilia from her mother Katrin and daring to humanise Katrin in her pain, sealed with a final kiss. Their disruptions of pageantry find echoes in Jed's wish to perforate the filmscreen of spectacle and complicity, but deny incorporation or absorption, unlike his attack on Alice. Jed, like Jack and Sandler and Bond's activists, operates at the level of pre-existent imagery and pseudo-rationality. Jed struggles and fails to find a suitable language of expression; Jack and Sandler find the physical a distraction from their Institution of rules of order; and the activists are open to misinterpretation until all the existing machinery of state interpretation has been transferred (*not* dismantled). Roche and Nelson defy interpretation and locate their power and motivation in speaking and being and hating: their imaginative resistance of reference points located outside their own respective cultures is therefore ultimately watertight. Barker's renegades of perception stage their revolt in the theatre of the body and the self, bypassing the abstractions with which Gildersleeve crippled Tully in *Credentials*. They break moulds of association to license the riot of possibilities, and are thus closest to Burroughs' Johnson Family in their essentially liberationist demonstrations of an obligation to prove that the world unlocks.

NOTES

1. *Magnificence* (London: Eyre Methuen, 1980), 48.
2. Ibid., 70.
3. See David Ian Rabey, *Howard Barker: Politics and Desire* (London: Macmillan, 1989), 3.
4. *Real Dreams* (London: Faber & Faber, 1987), 16.
5. Ibid., 29.
6. Ibid., 31.
7. Ibid., 53.
8. *The Worlds* (London: Eyre Methuen, 1980), 19.
9. Ibid., 25.
10. Ibid., 39.
11. Ibid., 83-4.
12. *Rat in the Skull* (London: Methuen, 1984), 9.
13. Ibid., 13.
14. Ibid., 23.
15. Ibid., 32.
16. *Credentials of a Sympathiser* (London: Calder, 1980), 74, 80.
17. Ibid., 81.

10

The Bomb in the Baby Carriage:
Women and Terrorism in Contemporary Drama

SUSANNE GREENHALGH

> The women say they have learned to rely on their own strength.
> They say they are aware of the force of their unity. They say, let
> those who call for a new language first learn violence. They say,
> let those who want to change the world first seize all the rifles.
> They say that they are starting from zero. They say a new world
> is beginning.
>
> Monique Wittig, *The Guérillères*, 1972[1]

In the 'ideological theater'[2] of patriarchal inscription, where masculine and feminine are opposed in such a way that the feminine invariably constitutes the weaker term, one of the most crucial binary oppositions of all is the gendering of war and peace.[3] An assumed historical association of women with nurturing and men with hunting and warfare has become the matrix for a 'collocation of "femininity", "peace" and "passivity" which is opposed in a delicate balance to a set comprising "masculinity", "war" and "activity" . . . enshrined in imagery, text, and social life, so that the relationship seems . . . natural and inevitable.'[4]

The extent to which terrorism can be considered a form of warfare is a matter of often bitter dispute, but it is clearly dominated by many of the same 'natural' symbols,[5] whether it is viewed as technique, strategem, or ideology, as a manifestation of age-old political violence or as a comparatively new historical phenomenon.[6] Analysts agree that violence is central and pervasive, categorising it as legitimate or illegitimate, rational or irrational, normal or deviant, according to their specific political persuasion. Action is paramount, and always intentionally and spectacularly aggressive. Whilst there is a strong emphasis on the protagonist role of the terrorist as

160

hero/martyr, an equal degree of instrumentalism is detected in relation to victims, who become doubly objectified – or desubjectified[7] – both by the threat to their lives and welfare, and by their use as unwilling actors in what is variously viewed as: a mode of symbolic action;[8] one version of the social dramas through which all societies transform or consolidate themselves;[9] a pragmatic means of transferring political power;[10] a genre of cultural narrative;[11] a dialogue with fathers;[12] or a form of violent language addressed to an enemy audience.[13]

There is general agreement on one matter, however: terrorism is a man's game[14]. The preferred qualities of violent activism, aggression, and willingness to make use of others all constitute terrorism as an extreme expression of militant machismo.[15] In her recent study of the power of the terrorist myth, Robin Morgan finds nothing abnormal in the male terrorist. He is in fact the 'logical incarnation of patriarchal politics in a technological world', and inherits the sexual charisma of the archetypal masculine hero/martyr, whose ecstatic, messianic self-dedication turns him into a weapon that, in Nechayev's words, will 'burst into the lives of the people'.[16] Women, by contrast, can only ever be 'token terrorists', masochistic victims of this demon lover, who seduces them into an alien world where they must appear 'fearsome, soulless, godforsaken creatures, symbols or cyphers',[17] unless they confine themselves to traditional feminine roles of service and self-sacrifice. As would-be leaders they can succeed only at the expense of their femininity, of their 'natural' selves, forced to give strained, artificial impersonations of men, or to become alienated misfits.[18]

If terrorism is a form of theatre, this is especially the case for women, cast fundamentally against type. So ingrained is the opposition of femininity and terrorism in the popular mind that the juxtaposition of images of 'normal' feminine domestic activity with the female terrorist's transgressive activism often provides a visual shorthand for films and other narratives that seek to establish terrorism's illegitimacy and unnaturalness.[19] Although there is a powerful popular tradition which makes the role-reversing 'woman on top' a symbol of revolution itself, she is always an ambivalent figure, regarded as potentially monstrous, an uncontrollable Fury who will devour all in her path, engulfing everything in rivers of blood.[20] Terrorism thus offers a classic example of the double-bind that patriarchy characteristically constructs for women. As Other, object, and victim, even in an arena that privileges violent protagonism, her activity will be judged to be intrinsically deviant or psychotic.

It is not simply its role-playing that makes terrorism akin to theatre, however. Dramatic action itself has traditionally been regarded as being structured from violent conflict and opposition.[21] Feminist analysis suggests that these linear, action-based narratives are inherently sadistic ones, in which, whatever their stage-gender, agents of action are always viewed as masculine and victims as feminine. If theatre is indeed a means by which human beings disguise, allay and control their fear of the other and the aggression it generates, it is no accident that the theatre anthropologist Eugenio Barba finds the most forceful image of the actor's relationship with otherness in the dancing, sword-wielding figure of a woman dressed as a warrior, an icon of transgression which ruptures and transforms that most fixed of cultural conventions, the difference between masculine and feminine.[22] It is equally significant, however, that this transvestism is male in form. The exploration of femininity through male cross-dressing, though a common feature of theatre, is itself a chief source of the 'anti-theatrical prejudice', a 'surface representation' attuned to masculine narcissistic desire, an occasion for laughter, or a means of control through parody.[23] When women assume the guise of the violent activist, in the theatre or in actuality, this will be most often seen as a form of perverse transvestism, a morbid rejection of her natural role as victim or as maternal giver and sustainer of life.

Toller's *Masse-Mensch* (*Man and the Masses*, 1921) encapsulates the traditional gender codings of revolutionary struggle:

> THE WOMAN: . . . I know who you are.
> 'Kill him,' you cried. Always your cry is 'Kill him!'
> Your father's name is War.
> You are his bastard.

You poor, new head-of-staff of executioners, Your only
remedy: 'Death!' and 'Shoot them down!'
The one who murders for the State,
You call an executioner.
But he who murders for mankind
Is called a saviour . . .
Yes, you can speak of good and holy violence . . .

THE NAMELESS ONE: You lack the power to face the
unyielding fact,
The need to act.
Free men will only come
Through hard facts and through harder deeds![24]

For the Woman, political violence is part of an endless cycle of
patriarchal murderousness, handed down from father to son,
to be halted only by choosing self-sacrifice above the killing
of others. For the nameless male her choice only confirms
both her essential political powerlessness and irrelevancy,
and her one value to the revolutionary cause as victim and
martyr. Similar symbolic patterns emerge even in those contemporary plays which apparently seek to portray women
not simply, as Brecht had it, embracing the butcher, but
taking on the butcher's role themselves. In Howard Brenton's
Magnificence (1973) the prospect and failure of revolutionary
change is embodied in the pregnancy and violence-induced
miscarriage of one of the activists, inevitably named Mary.[25]
Howard Barker's play sequence *The Possibilities* (1987) creates
a universe of terror in which a woman's instincts of trust and
humanity lead her to open the door to the terrorists who
kill her husband. Instructed that 'to survive we must learn
everything we had forgotten, and unlearn everything we
were taught, and being inhuman, overcome inhumanity' she
applies the lesson by attempting to kill her child – but cannot
bring herself to do so. If motherhood is made the opposite
of murder in these plays Edward Bond's *The Worlds* (1976)
presents female terrorists who are sinister maternal parodies
feeding a helpless, swaddled hostage: '[*She cradles the white
figure and pushes the end of the tube through a hole in the hood. It
feeds. She nurses it and tidies its clothes*]'.[26] As René Girard and
Julia Kristeva have argued, in the sacrificial, scapegoating

procedures and institutions, from war to theatre, evolved
to control the potentially endless 'violent reciprocity' of rival
masculine subjects, the threat of absolute power and absolute
violence may be displaced onto the feminine through the myth
of the murderous, devouring mother, who embodies return
to an infantile non-differentiation and self-dissolution both
desired and feared, the 'empty space' of the pre-Symbolic that
theatre and all other signifying practices seek to occupy.[27]

For Kristeva, that maternal empty space is also utopia.[28]
Terrorism may indeed be a key expression of the violence of
patriarchy but in its revolutionary form it also dreams of the
possibility of a new world. All the plays discussed below, each
concerned in some way with women's involvement in terrorism, analyse the relationship between violence and politics in
the light of changing concepts of gender roles. All recognise
that there is a 'bomb in the baby carriage' and that the central
icon of motherhood can no longer naturalise and thus stabilise
a world dominated by masculine violence. Through a variety
of forms, in diverse cultural and political contexts, all employ
the world-building powers of theatre to explore the possible
engendering of that new world.

The past and present violence that marks the history of Northern Ireland has, according to Rob Richie, caused its playwrights to turn back to 'polluted origins to search into the
roots of a society so impregnated with strife and division'.[29]
The gendering of the metaphor is significant. Analysis of
both the consequences and the possible causes of the conflict have led feminists to term Northern Ireland an 'armed
patriarchy' in which the cult of violent virility makes political
and domestic brutality both ubiquitous and inseparable in
a society where rigid sex-role divisions are maintained by
economic conditions and by ideology.[30] A long history of
'faction-fights', combined with nationalist mystique, religious
fears, and 'free-floating aggression', within a predominently
working-class community, still ensure an audience for the
philosophy of Padraig Pearse: 'Bloodshed is a cleansing and
satisfactory thing and the nation which regards it as a final horror has lost its manhood.'[31] Within both nationalist and loyalist
groups, until quite recently, women tended to be regarded as

non-combatants, and were not targeted in sectarian killings.[32] Even when active in paramilitary groups they rarely played a leading role in terrorism but were in general restricted to traditional modes of female participation in revolutionary struggle, as couriers, providers of safehouses, look-outs, and decoys. Their political involvement has largely been directed towards collective action in the community, from 'dust-bin lid' warnings to peace initiatives across the sectarian divide in the name of a common motherhood.

Although Ireland itself was theatrically feminised by Yeats as Cathleen ni Houlihan, whose old woman's shape disguises the seductive beauty which inspires young men to fight, the contrast of feminine non-violence with the vainglorious verbal and physical aggression of men has been a potent Irish stage tradition since O'Casey. The power of the mother opposes the would-be hard men, but equally characteristic is the figure of the young girl who falls sacrificial victim to masculine violence, as in the climax of *The Shadow of a Gunman*. Some recent plays by women have explored the political implications of these familiar gender attributions. In Christina Reid's *Joyriders* (1987), for instance, the final moments of O'Casey's play are used as a frame for an action which demonstrates the futility of such romantic stereotypes as any kind of solution to the troubles of present-day Ireland by amalgamating mother and seduced girl into one pathetic figure, cut down by cross-fire. Anne Devlin's investigation of the 'polluted origins' of Irish violence, whilst also concerned with the mother's role, explores the psychosexual dimension of the lives of women 'caught up in conflict' . As this phrase suggests, her women characters are depicted as passive victims of a history they cannot control, even when they are themselves agents of terrorist violence. The theme of betrayal which Laqueur notes as a characteristic feature of terrorist fiction here takes the form of often melodramatically-plotted portrayals of the terrorist as a 'demon lover' who takes possession of his victims.[34] Sectarian violence is thus traced in the sexual identities, as well as the sexual politics, of her characters.

For the women in Devlin's plays, the history of Ireland is a suffocating dream of violence initiated and carried out by men, unsparingly revealed in the 'gradual and deliberate processes' that 'weave their way in the dark corners of all our rooms'.[35] Like the psychiatrist (and possible sex-murderer) in the television play *A Woman Calling* (BBC 2 1982, published 1986) they are sensitive to 'the tyranny of dreams . . . in particular the power of dreams to cast a spell over a life', forced to ask 'whose dreams do we dream? . . . what fatal smoke inhale unwittingly from a distant fire . . .': 'the pain we feel is real pain, we know it – it constricts our breathing . . . we are infected and we remain infected . . . our crisis is past, but we go on dreaming it.'[36]

Finn, in Devlin's radio and television play *Naming the Names* (BBC Radio 4, 1986, BBC 2 1987), who is fated in the name of a male hero of legend and becomes an IRA activist, can only 'glimpse what fatal visions stir that web's dark pattern'. Caught like a fly in a history first spun in childhood from her grandmother's tales of the Easter Rising she only recognises what her own role has been at the end of a sequence of tragic events. Betrayed by her British lover she in turn lures a young protestant with whom she has fallen in love into an assassination trap. Nightmares of suffocation and strangulation are physicalised in actual epileptic fits, and political involvement, seen as inseparable from sexual involvement, is signalled by a succession of slammed and locked doors. Even the park, with its liberating images of seasonal change, children playing, and flowing water, is the location for her victim's death. The play ends with Finn taking refuge, under interrogation, in a childhood skipping game, 'naming the names' of the streets of Belfast, which themselves commemorate an imperialistic military past and encode the maze of a violent history from which there seems no escape.

In *Ourselves Alone* (1986) Devlin offers only two ways out: exile, or refuge in motherhood as an attempt to break the cycle of tribal violence by changing the formative experiences of the child. Alternating private domestic space with the public worlds of the streets and the political bars, in a largely naturalistic mode the play consistently employs personal, and especially sexual, possessiveness and betrayal to underline the issue of gender in the repeated assertion that 'there are no differences between one person and another that are not personal' (23). Three women, born into or closely connected with a patriarchically-ruled Provisional IRA family, spend their lives 'waiting on men' who are either in prison, committed to other women, or on the wrong political side; all in a sense thus 'demon lovers', their seductive exteriors concealing at best infidelity, at worst personal and political violence and treachery. The women's existence is not only darkened by shadows of the gunmen but by all the other male figures who have dominated their lives since infancy:

> We grew up by the hearth and slept in cots by the fire. We escaped nothing and nothing escaped us. . . . I wish I could go back . . . somehow rid myself of that dark figure which hovered about the edge of my cot – priest or police I can't tell – but the light is so dim in my memory – most of the room is in shadow – and – gets dimmer all the time . . . the first few moments when I took the wrong way. (78)

The speaker is Josie, an IRA courier, who once wanted to 'take the same risks as a man' and planted a car-bomb, but has now 'lost the killing instinct' and believes 'the crushing of a foetus a tragedy' (63). Made pregnant by an Englishman who turns out to be a spy, Josie refuses to have the abortion her Provo brother demands, and thus has no option but to accept the protection of the father she has tried to escape, ensuring that this child, too, will grow up in the shadows. Frieda, ambitious to be a singer and rewrite the classic republican songs from a woman's point of view, has her voice stifled both by sectarian censorship and her Protestant lover, whose Marxism doesn't prevent him from battering her both physically and mentally to keep her as his sexual property. As in *Naming the Names*, this political and personal possessiveness has physical symptoms. Donna, who has left husband and child for a man whose terrorist convictions have kept him in jail for most of their lives together, suffers asthma attacks and dreams that a devil, who is also her jealous lover, is suffocating her. All the women remember a lost mother who once protected them, but Donna's daughter, in a house always liable to military search, already has 'wee dreams' and wakes in the night. Motherhood is not celebrated as a safe haven but is rather seen as a blind leap into another kind of darkness:

'I felt for the first time the course of things, the inevitability. And I thought, no, I won't struggle any more, I shall just do' (89).

The real celebration comes in the final moments of the play, in Frieda's evocation of a time of freedom long ago, when, during a moonlit, seaside barbecue, the three girls escaped from the men arguing around the fire and swam naked in the calm, phosphorescent water. The cool brightness of this archetypically feminine element is juxtaposed with the 'fatal smoke' of the bonfire around which political debate is hardening into division. It is this recollection of 'ourselves alone' that offers refuge from the possession of violent men and their history. In the 'great hatred, little room' of Northern Ireland, where a wife-beater like Bobby Sands is a hero if he dies a martyr to the cause, Devlin's plays counter Yeats's diagnosis that fanaticism is innate, engendered in the mother's womb, and instead shows the impact of 'what we saw through the bars of a cot or heard from a corner of a nursery that made us what we are (78).[37] Nevertheless, this stress on the personal leaves the conventional gendering of political violence essentially intact. The women's instincts for non-violence are linked with their femininity and, especially, their maternal potential.

The growing prominence of women in the aggressive European terrorism of the seventies had already challenged such assumptions. Figures like Ulrike Meinhof, both a playwright who wrote of violent female rebellion and a mother prepared to give up her children to the revolutionary struggle, prompted experiment with non-naturalistic forms. In work by the Italian performer and left-wing activist Franca Rame and the East German playwright Heiner Müller, terrorism becomes an arena for a committed exploration of 'the man–woman relationship of today'[38] which results, on the one hand, in the reworking of traditional popular forms for revolutionary effect and, on the other, in the shattering of naturalistic modes of presentation in the service of a pessimistic vision that despairs of radical change.

If Devlin's plays reveal a political world outside the control of women, three of Rame's monologues *Io, Ulrike, Grido* (*I, Ulrike, Cry*, premiered 1977, published 1978), *Tomorrow's News*

(1978), and *La Madre* (*The Mother*, premiered 1982, published 1983),[39] fuse theatrical and political agency into a powerful re-examination of female roles. Although the first two were scripted in collaboration with her husband, Dario Fo, all have been developed by Rame in performance, and indeed form part of a movement out of his artistic and political shadow, into the autonomy of a one-woman show, *Tutta casa, letto e chiesa* (*She's all home, bed and church/Female Parts*). In general terms they can be viewed as emerging from the terrorism-dominated political troubles of Italy in the seventies but more specifically they are the outcome of Rame's leading role in the organisation Sorccorso Rosso (Red Aid), an offshoot of Fo/Rame's theatre company La Commune, which, between 1972 and 1977, initiated and coordinated assistance for the families of prisoners jailed under anti-terrorism legislation and campaigned for their human rights in the face of the often brutal conditions in which they were kept. In 1973, as a direct result of her political activities, Rame was the subject of magisterial investigation, and suffered abduction, rape, and physical abuse by a neo-fascist group, an experience upon which she later based *Lo Strupo* (*The Rape/I Don't Move, I Don't Scream, My Voice is Gone . . .* , 1983).[40]

Rame grew up in an family of itinerant professional actors who preserved something of the *commedia dell'arte* heritage in their ability to *recitare a soggetto* or improvise from a situation through highly disciplined if stereotyped gestural performance, which was yet free to respond to the reactions of changing audiences.[41] In her work with Fo this mode of acting has come closer to Brechtian *gestus*, conducting an audience through a succession of different perspectives on a situation, as though watching the changing shots of a camera.[42] Although technically monologues, the pieces are intrinsically dialogic, since all the different characters are fully realised in voice, gesture, and movement. As a theatrical form they are thus particularly empowering for a female performer, allowing her sole occupation of the stage whilst also enabling her to appropriate masculine elements without assuming male disguise or identification. In Rame's own performances she is able to manipulate both the feminine 'mask' acquired through her family training and her experience as

'object of the male gaze' in filmwork. If, for Rame, 'the
best way to act a tragedy' is 'to take it to the limit of the
grotesque'[43] the radical, revolutionary potential embodied in
popular traditions of the 'grotesque' transgressive woman
becomes a way not only of dramatising the tragedy of Italian
terrorism but also of projecting in fantasy a possible utopian
solution.

Both *Io, Ulrike, Grido* and *Tomorrow's News* exploit feminist theories of women as victim and object of a masculine
gaze that is sadistic in its desire; they succeed, however, in
transforming the viewed woman into an emblem of victory. *Io,
Ulrike, Grido*, based on Meinhof's own words and premiered
to commemorate the first anniversary of her death, shows
her in her isolation cell at Stammheim, on the eve of what
is presented as her murder. In her timeless 'tomb of silence.
White silence . . . an aquarium' (47–8), Ulrike is a latter-day
Antigone, and the act of speech itself becomes a gesture of
struggle and resistance to the torture of sensory deprivation
and constant surveillance. Like the actress for her audience,
Meinhof is a spectacle for her jailors: 'I see you squashing
your noses up against the thick glass of this aquarium where
you've put me to float around, observing me with interest.
You enjoy the spectacle.'

Spectacle is central to the piece's political analysis of the
'beautiful world' of capitalism: 'outside you've painted your
grey, decaying world in gaudy colours, and lured people to
consume every conceivable colour . . . You even paint up your
women like motley clowns . . . You make a great spectacle
of high security, but its only fear that makes you so cruel
and deranged. That's why you need a non-stop spectacle
of noise, coloured neon, lights everywhere' (48). Against
this annulment of identity and the counterfeit carnival of
the State, Meinhof asserts the festive, revolutionary laughter
of the oppressed and the witch, using the radical energies of
the performing body to conjure up the 'hubble bubble' of the
production lines, echoing the pandemonium of capitalism
back on itself through an anarchic, parodic deployment of
the actor's full physical resources: 'Press: fluuuttsss . . .
Hammer: blamm . . . Drill: frufrufru . . . Engine: popopo
. . . Cauldron: ploch . . . ploch . . .'(49).

In deliberate counterpoint *Tomorrow's News* imagines another victory of female voice and body, but no laughter, in the projected survival of Irmgard Moeller, an intended Stammheim victim, whose resuscitation exposes the 'pseudo-terrorism' of a State ready to use its prisoners' bodies as weapons in a ruthless propaganda war. With its graphic presentation of the experience of being brutally and clinically killed – a process at one point likened to an abortion – it is comparable with *Lo Strupo* in its power to subvert familiar stage conventions of feminine victimisation and demand audience identification whilst simultaneously maintaining an integral distance and control. At the end of *Io, Ulrike, Grido* the political importance of this stress on women's experience is encapsulated by the rewriting of Meinhof's own quotation of Mao, 'Weightier than the Tai Mountain is the death of a socialist fighter': 'My death is gargantuan, like a mountain . . . Thousands and thousands of women's arms have raised up this immense mountain, and let it fall with a hideous laugh' (50). A carnivalesque tradition of highly physicalised performance combined with what is almost a form of Marxist martyr's play powerfully and literally embodies the utopian prospect of a women's revolution.

La Madre also combines direct appeals to audience empathy with excursions into fantasy: 'I . . . I don't just need your attention: most of all I need your imagination.' Based on the testimonies of women helped by Sorccorso Rosso, it dramatises the situation of a mother who learns from the TV news that her son is a terrorist and as a result stops being a 'letter-box' for society's ideas and becomes capable, in dream at least, of decisive action. Unlike the deliberately claustrophobic prison dramas *La Madre* employs a varied temporal and spatial structure to present terrorism in its full complexity, in order to awaken Italians to the reality of state repression and make them aware that terrorism is no aberration but the logical outcome of a violent, sick society. It is in effect a crash course in the political history of recent years seen through the initially naive eyes of that central icon of Italian culture, the mother. Inevitably she starts by blaming her own poor mothering: 'I breast-fed him, I cuddled him . . . but he has turned out violent.' Gradually, however, she traces the connections between the failures of the revolutionary idealism of the sixties, emblematised in the poster of a young Vietnamese girl standing guard over a hulking US pilot, the neo-fascist backlash of the seventies, and a general social malaise that produces drug addiction as well as terrorism in the young. When she finally visits her son in jail, she is confronted with evidence of the state's brutality in the form of strip-searches and the beating of prisoners.

Finally she dreams that 'those bastards who made up the motherhood myth' sit in judgement on her and her child. When offered a deal in exchange for naming names, any names, that will keep the witch-hunt going, the mother naively questions the danger of prosecuting innocent people, and, like Alice in the Court of Wonderland, she causes a 'blow-up' of the proceedings. Able at last to see beneath its facade to the tortured body of her son, she hands him back to the authorities in the piece's final, and shocking, *gestus*, as a dead body: 'I held him too tight . . . I strangled him'. With this final fusion of Medea (another of Rame's monologues) and the *pietà*, Rame uses traditional feminine images to subvert the 'motherhood myth' and display its manipulation by a repressive state that cannot conceal its own violence. David Hirst considers the piece a critique of left-wing politics unlikely to cause the right much discomfort.[44] However, it is the perspectives of feminism, not a rejection of radicalism, that shape Rame's awareness of the inadequacies of Marxist analysis and the need to theorise and realise a revolution for women as well as men.

According to some critics, these pieces are 'direct cries from the heart unmediated by any paraphernalia of dramatic representation' that 'bypass the necessity of intellectual argumentation'.[45] Emotion is indeed vital to Rame's work but the aesthetic control of her juxtaposition of different forms of female experience with parodies of male authoritarianism make it a much more subtle theatrical art than these comments suggest. In her terrorism pieces, through their emphasis both on specifically female experiences of oppression and resistance and on the tragedy and farce of political violence, Rame provides an analysis that sets the personal and the political in dialectical relation.

Ulrike Meinhof and Medea are also central to Heiner Müller's *Hamlet-machine* (1977) but they are employed to negate
rather than embody the possibility of revolution. Müller's
theatre of terrorism does not abandon the Oedipal drama
of pyschic victimisation or the Brechtian theatre of dialectic
but rather explodes both into a new kind of apocalyptic
performance spectacle that deliberately resists 'conceptual
formulation . . . and cannot be reduced to one-dimensional
metaphor', yoking images violently together in the manner of
Eisensteinian cinematic montage or Elizabethan poetry, 'as a
kind of visual protection against a too rapidly changing reality' (138).

On the 'eve of the century of Orestes and Electra that's rising', which will make Oedipus appear a comedy (29), *Hamlet-
machine* in a sense theatricalises Hélène Cixous's hypothesis:
'And suppose there is no Orestes anymore? And suppose
Electra was going to kill? What if women took over from
men, made off with the scepter, the dagger. . . . That would
mean that there are manly possibilities in woman. That the
reign of mothers is therefore not dead, that power could
come again from the direction of the maternal hearth.'[46] This
is done at one remove, however, through a reworking of the
Orestean/Oedipal revenge tragedy of *Hamlet*, 'a drama that
doesn't happen anymore', along with revolutions, in which
Ophelia becomes both the real protagonist and a 'criticism of
Hamlet' (80). Amid 'the ruins of Europe' (53), dead landscape
of pollution and technological debris whose 'tomorrow has
been cancelled' (54) a Freudian 'family scrapbook' is juxtaposed with evocations of the failure of the Hungarian uprising. Destruction of the author's own photograph by 'the actor
playing Hamlet', who refuses to perform his role, is paralleled
by an onslaught on the mythic figures of communist thought,
Marx, Lenin, and Mao, by an 'actor of Hamlet' who has
stepped into his dead father's armour (58). If the stage space is
a scene of desolation from the start the action largely consists
of further acts of demolition. The 'Europe of Women', sce-
nically an 'enormous room' which exaggerates and parodies
the familiar domestic settings of naturalistic drama in which
scenarios of feminine victimisation are enacted, is destroyed
by Ophelia. The final images are of nuclear winter, and a

dead sea, in which 'fish, debris, dead bodies, and limbs drift by' (58).

Transvestism surfaces briefly as a visual motif without unleashing any liminal energies for real change. Not only does the actor playing Hamlet refuse to act in any sense of the word, he initially rejects the 'fearful armor' of masculinity – 'I want to be a woman' (55), 'I don't want to kill anymore' (57) – and dresses in drag in Ophelia's clothes. Ophelia/Ulrike (who is also Müller's wife who committed suicide in 1966), after a mocking striptease, stops killing *herself* and becomes the avenger Electra/Ulrike: 'I destroy the battlefield that was my home . . . I walk into the streets clothed in my blood.' (54–5). But Müller himself regards the work as an exorcism of nightmare, rather than a millenarian vision, 'the description of a petrified hope, an effort to articulate a despair so that it can be left behind' (50). When the female figure speaks the final words of the play she is immobilised in a wheelchair, swathed in white gauze by male medics:

> This is Electra speaking . . . In the name of the victims. I eject all the sperm I have received. I turn the milk of my breasts into lethal poison. I take back the world I gave birth to. I choke between my thighs the world I gave birth to. I bury it in my womb. Down with the happiness of submission. Long live hate and contempt, rebellion and death. When she walks through your bedrooms carrying butcher's knives you'll know the truth. (58)

The last line, taken from the words of another murderous woman, Squeaky Fromme, would-be presidential assassin and member of the Manson gang, most notorious for its killing of the pregnant actress Sharon Tate, holds out no comfort in a 'reign of mothers'. As Bonnie Marranca points out, women's bodies are simultaneously utopian landscapes, devastated colonies, and devouring black holes in Müller's work, but are always 'like nature made to embody the ideology of the eternal feminine, passive, fated'.[47] Here the destiny of the maternal is both to destroy and to be destroyed. In the first sequence Hamlet states that 'Women should be sewed up – a world without mothers. We could butcher each other in peace and quiet . . .' (53). If motherhood is here synonymous with non-violence, later an icon of the madonna appears with the pierced heart of maternal suffering replaced by a breast cancer that 'radiates like the sun' of a nuclear explosion (55). Ophelia's inversion of procreation into slaughter becomes both the necessary first step 'TO OVERTHROW ALL EXISTING CONDITIONS' (58) and a final gesture of despair.

In Marranca's view Müller has put women on the stage of history in uniquely strong roles, and made Ulrike Meinhof 'the female protagonist in the last drama of the bourgeois world'[48] but in a drama in which there is 'no historical substance for real dialogues' (50), the separate monologues of Ophelia and Hamlet reveal not simply women capable of violence but also men who still desire dissolution in and *of* the Mother and the earth she symbolises. Whereas Rame's Medean mother exposes the political consequences of the motherhood myth, Müller's work remains dominated by it. To assign world-destroying impulses to a female figure appears in the end no path to revolution but merely another form of cross-dressing in order to control, a species of male transvestism amounting to travesty, a disengendering which leaves crucial aspects of masculinity intact, and can hold out no prospect of the fundamental transformation that the world's – or the theatre's – regeneration requires.

Trevor Griffiths' *Real Dreams* (1987), a theatrical rewriting of Jeremy Pikser's fiction 'Revolution in Cleveland', is also inspired by a terrorist group dominated by women, that involved in the Nyack Brinks robbery of 1981.[49] The 'man-woman relationship of today' is again at the centre of a male dramatist's analysis of both the prospect and the means for revolution, and, like Müller's, Griffiths' intertextuality can be viewed as a form of masculine self-critique. The chosen theatrical mode, however, is an ironically modulated naturalism, fractured persistently by non-illusionistic direct address or interior monologue, in which domestic setting and detail are employed to contextualise an interrogation of the impact of the 'natural' binary oppositions of gender on ideals of unified revolutionary struggle. *Real Dreams* shows the consequences of 'bringing the war back home' on the revolutionary politics of both men and women but never questions, however, the primacy of the martial metaphor itself.

Such a critique is central to the work of the British play-wright Caryl Churchill. Terrorism has been treated in a numb-er of her plays but always in the context of the relationship between personal and political violence, and the complex symbiosis between state modes of control and the subversive counter-violence these provoke.[50] As a feminist she seeks 'to avoid the danger of a static polarization of women as peaceful and men as violent' by dramatising the 'capacity for violence' of both sexes.[51] *Objections to Sex and Violence* (1985), written before the advent of the Red Army Faction or a sustained IRA offensive, explores anarchistic revolutionary violence in terms of women's involvement in groups such as the Angry Brigade and the Symbionese Liberation Army.[52] As the now-preferred title, *Bread and Circuses*, suggests, however, the play is equally concerned with the 'soft controls' that society employs to maintain the status quo, and with responses to the spectacle of suffering. Set in a characteristic liminal locale of feminist drama, on the seashore, between low and high tide, its two acts mingle diverse groups of friends, relations, and strangers, some portrayed naturalistically, others deliberately cartoon-like, in a series of casual and violent encounters. Apparently loosely-structured to the point of inconsequentiality, its quasi-choric form can be viewed as variations on a Reichian theme, that of the link between sexuality and violence.

Jule and her lover Eric, on the run after an unspecified terrorist action, debate the use of violence to bring about revolutionary change: 'What's the most obvious difference it makes? A bit of rubble and perhaps a few people not walking along that were walking along somewhat happy' (37). Their politics have emerged from the often frightening experiments with living and loving undergone with another couple in a col-lective household. Retreating from the extremism of some of the resulting relationships, Eric dreams of a revolution which would emerge simply from the process of change in oneself and others: 'Why can't I think of my life as a slow explosion into other lives, not hurting but somehow changing –' (37). In contrast, Jule tries to persuade her sister Annie and lover Phil, whose rage and frustration is repressed in physical symptoms or aggression against each other, to take violent revenge on the bosses for whom 'all of us are just things . . . And being hurt is all they notice'. With the appearance at the end of the play of Jule's ex-husband, Terry, a dedicated communist who now cares for their child, the conflict between control, even the self-control of a revolutionary movement, and an anarchism committed to the violence of human desire, is made explicit:

JULE: How's your sex life these days?
TERRY: Secondary.
JULE: Like violence is secondary?
TERRY: Yes, if you like. They're both distractions from work that has to be done. Secondary and confusing.
JULE: You should pay it more attention.
TERRY: I should pay it less. (45)

Further examples of repression appear in the bizarre conjunction of a Mary Whitehouse caricature with the cliché flasher in a dirty raincoat, one believing that 'public services should force the public' into morality, the other that sexual 'self-service could mean yourself using force' (18). A disturbed elderly spinster roams the dunes seeking the site of an erotic encounter she rejected long ago. When Jule asks her what she would do with explosives, in a graphic equation of the themes of explosion, orgasm, and self-destruction that have run through the play, she answers 'I'd throw it – I'd throw it – No I'd hold it tight against myself, and there [hand on vagina] at last' (29). Later Phil, who once tried to sleep with Jule and still desires her, responds to her urgings to 'say no' to the system, by throwing petrol onto a fire as she bends over it. The impulse to see 'how things blaze up' (33) is contrasted with the cold, efficient violence that Terry represents and advocates, which would lead him, in Jule's words, to rape 'only if ordered. But if ordered, very thoroughly' (47).

The play resists conclusions as it does consistency of form. Personal and political violence are brought into relationship but never quite equated. Neither are they consistently gendered. Like the storm that interrupts the sunshine in which most of the action takes place, violence erupts in all the characters, in ideological, sexual, or familial confrontations. Although it is Jule's presence which has summoned up some of these encounters she is no protagonist, for the play itself is a dramatisation of the need to find a solution other than the

mode of tragic action to the material and psychic suffering
of the world. In the last moments, she and Terry, who is
dressed for a funeral, talk of inevitable death and dissolution,
the killing of a dog in a road accident, and an old man's heart
attack. She will not return to her role as mother but, in any
case, Terry has taken her place, and for this night at least they
will be lovers and not opponents. In a play full of violent acts
but without what would normally be recognised as dramatic
action, the ending, in silence and stasis, might be interpreted
as signalling, like the end of *Hamlet-machine* or 'Revolution in
Cleveland', the defeat of revolutionary idealism. But they also
sit in sunshine by the shore of a still living, changing sea. They
do not see themselves as victims of history, but the changes
they have undergone, the 'slow explosions' of intense personal relationships and altering gender roles, force them to ask
what kind of activism can best change the world. *Objections
to Sex and Violence* ultimately leaves both question and answer
with its audience.

Julia Kristeva notes that 'since the dawn of feminism, and certainly beyond, the political activity of exceptional women, and
thus in a certain sense of liberated women, has taken the form
of murder, conspiracy, and crime'. Kristeva detects, however,
a possessed, paranoid, and sacrificial counter-investment in
masculine violence in such patterns.[53]

> If the archetype of the belief in a good and pure sub-
> stance, that of utopias, is the belief in the omnipotence of
> an archaic, full, total, englobing mother with no frustra-
> tion, no separation with no break-producing symbolism
> (with no castration, in other words), then it becomes
> evident that we will never be able to defuse the violences
> mobilized through the counterinvestment necessary to
> carrying out this phantasm, unless one challenges pre-
> cisely this myth of the archaic mother.[54]

All the plays examined, to varying degrees, engage with
the relationship between 'the terror of power and terrorism
as desire for power' in the context of maternal symbolism.
All carry out some kind of analysis of 'the potentialities of
victim/executioner which characterize each identity, each subject, each sex'. They all thus contribute in some part to what

Kristeva terms the 'de-dramatization' of the '"fight to the death" between rival groups and thus between the sexes',[55] the *agon* which has shaped cultural as well as theatrical form for so much of human history. In the process all have moved, to some extent at least, in the direction of theatrical experiment, if only via a rejection of naturalism as an adequate form for portraying a world where what is 'natural' is constantly in question. Terrorism may be the contemporary expression of that ancient 'fight to the death' but in contemporary drama it also becomes a field for challenging the very foundations of such myths. The bomb in the baby carriage has already exploded and theatre is recording its impact.

NOTES

1. Monique Wittig, *The Guérillères*, trans. David Le Vay (London: Picador, 1972), 90.
2. Hélène Cixous, 'Sorties', in Hélène Cixous and Catherine Clément, *The Newly-Born Woman* trans. Betsy Wing, *Theory and History of Literature*, Vol. 24 (Manchester: Manchester University Press, 1986), 83.
3. See Anthony Wilden, *Man and Woman, War and Peace: The Strategist's Companion* (London: Routledge Kegan Paul, 1987).
4. Sharon Macdonald, Pat Holden, and Shirley Ardener, eds., *Images of Women in War and Peace: Cross-Cultural and Historical Perspectives* (London: Macmillan in association with Oxford University Women's Studies Committee, 1987), 21. See also Nancy Huston, 'The Matrix of War: Mothers and Heroes', in Susan Rubin Suleiman, ed., *The Female Body in Western Culture: Contemporary Perspectives* (Cambridge, Mass.: Harvard University Press, 1985), 119-36.
5. According to Stephen Segaller, *Invisible Armies: Terrorism into the 1990s* (London: Michael Joseph, 1986), 11, terrorism is not war because it is not subject to conventions, whilst for Andrew C. Janos, 'Authority and Violence: The Political Framework of Internal War', in Harry Eckstein, ed., *Internal War: Problems and Approaches* (New York: Free Press, 1964), 130-41, it is akin to military force as a means of transferring authority (132). In Paul Wilkinson's view it is a 'special form of clandestine, undeclared ... warfare waged without any humanitarian restraints or rules'; see 'Terrorism versus Liberal Democracy: The Problem of

Response', in William Gutteridge, ed., *The New Terrorism* (London: Institute for the Study of Conflict, 1986), 3. Klaus Wasmund, in 'The Political Socialization of West German Terrorists', in Peter H. Merkl, ed., *Political Violence and Terror: Motifs and Motivations* (London and Berkeley: University of California Press, 1986), 191-228, notes the key role played by the terms 'fight', 'fighter', and 'to fight' in the vocabulary of terrorists themselves (216), and according to the psychologist Franco Ferracuti, all terrorism is a form of 'fantasy war' (cited in Merkl, 52).

6. See Walter Laqueur, *The Age of Terrorism* (London: Weidenfeld and Nicholson, 1987); Paul Wilkinson and Alisdair Stewart, eds., *Contemporary Research on Terrorism* (Aberdeen: Aberdeen University Press, 1987); Wolfgang J. Mommsen and Gerhard Hirschfeld, eds., *Social Protest, Violence, and Terror in Nineteenth and Twentieth Century Europe* (London: Macmillan for the German Historical Institute, 1982); Noel O'Sullivan, ed., *Terrorism, Ideology, and Revolution* (Brighton: Harvester, 1986); John Richard Thackrah *Encyclopedia of Terrorism and Political Violence* (London: Routledge Kegan Paul, 1987); Juliet Lodge, *The Threat of Terrorism* (Sussex: Wheatsheaf, 1988). See also Segaller, Eckstein, Gutteridge, and Merkl, cited above.

7. Robin Wagner-Pacifici, *The Moro Morality Play: Terrorism as Social Drama*, (Chicago: University of Chicago Press, 1986), x.

8. Thomas Perry Thornton, 'Terror as Weapon' in Eckstein, 73.

9. Wagner-Pacifici, *passim*.

10. E. V. Walter, *Terror and Resistance: A Study of Political Violence with Case Studies of Some Primitive African Communities*, Terror and Society 1 (New York: Oxford University Press, 1969), 346.

11. Khachig Tololyan, 'Cultural Narrative and the Motivation of the Terrorist', in David C. Rapoport, ed., *Inside Terrorist Organizations* (London: Frank Cass, 1988), 217.

12. Jerrold Post, cited in Peter H. Merkl, 'Approaches to the Study of Political Violence', in Merkl, 79.

13. Alex P. Schmid and Jenny de Graaf, *Violence as Communication: Insurgent Terrorism and the Western News Media* (London and California: Sage Publications, 1982), 1-2.

14. See, for instance Laqueur, 79-80; Thackrah, 287-8. For studies of women as terrorists see David E. Georges-Abeyie, 'Women as Terrorists', in Laurence Freedman and Yonah Alexander, eds., *Perspectives in Terrorism* (Wilmington, Del.: Scholarly Resources, 1983), 71-4; William Lee Eubank and Leonard Weinberg, 'Italian Women Terrorists', *Terrorism* 9, no. 3 (1987): 241-62; H. H. A. Cooper,

'Women as Terrorists', in Freda Adler and Rita James Simon, eds., *The Criminology of Deviant Women* (Boston: Houghton Mifflin, 1979), 150-7; Deborah M. Galvin, 'The Female Terrorist: A Socio-Psychological Perspective', *Behavioral Sciences and the Law* 1:2 (1983): 19-32.

15. See Merkl, 10, 58; F. Gentry Harris, 'Hypothetical Facets or Ingredients of Terrorism', *Terrorism* 3, no. ¾ (1980): 240 ff. On the significance of masculine 'instrumentalism' see Jessica Benjamin, 'The Bonds of Love: Rational Violence and Erotic Domination', *Feminist Studies* 6, no. 1 (Spring 1980): 144-74, and Deborah Cameron and Elizabeth Frazer, *The Lust to Kill: A Feminist Investigation of Sexual Murder* (London: Polity Press, 1987).

16. Robin Morgan, *The Demon Lover: On the Sexuality of Terrorism* (London: Methuen, 1989), 16, 21, 24, 33, 176-7.

17. Galvin, 21.

18. Cooper, 155.

19. Peter Schlesinger, Graham Murdock and Philip Elliott, *Televising Terrorism: Political Violence in Popular Culture* (London: Comedia, 1983), 93.

20. See Natalie Zemon Davis, 'Women on Top', *Society and Culture in Early Modern France* (London: Polity Press, 1987), 124-51; Klaus Theweleit, *Male Fantasies* Vol 1, *Women, Floods, Bodies, History*, trans. Stephen Conway with Erica Carter and Chris Turner (London: Polity Press, 1987).

21. See Julian Hilton, *Performance* (London: Macmillan, 1987), 146.

22. See Laura Mulvey, 'Visual Pleasure and Narrative Pleasure', *Screen* 16:3 (Autumn 1975); Teresa de Lauretis, 'The Violence of Rhetoric: Considerations on Representation and Gender', in *Technologies of Gender: Essays on Theory, Film, and Fiction* (Bloomington and Indianapolis: Indiana University Press, 1987), 31-50; Hélène Cixous, 'Aller à la mer', trans. Barbara Kerslake, *Modern Drama* (December 1984): 546-8; Jay Cantor, 'History as Theater: or Terror and Sacrifice' in *The Space Between: Literature and Politics* (Baltimore and London: Johns Hopkins University Press, 1981), 87-8; Herbert Blau, *Take Up the Bodies: Theater at the Vanishing Point* (Urbana: University of Illinois Press, 1982); Michael Goldman, The *Actor's Freedom: Toward a Theory of Drama* (New York: Viking, 1975); Eugenio Barba, 'Theatre Anthropology', in *Beyond the Floating Islands* (New York: PAJ Publications, 1986), 153-4.

23. See Jonas Barish, *The Anti-Theatrical Prejudice* (Berkeley: University of California Press, 1981); Peggy Phelan, 'Feminist Theory, Poststructuralism, and Performance', *The Drama Review* 32:1 (Spring 1988): 109-10; Mary Anne Doane, 'Film and the Masquerade – Theorising the

Female Spectator', *Screen* 23, no. 3-4 (Sept.-Oct. 1982): 81; Laurence Senelick, 'Changing Sex in Public: Female Impersonation as Performance Theatre, *Theater* XX (Spring 1989): 6-11; Ann Herrmann, 'Travesty and Transgression in Shakespeare, Brecht, and Churchill', *Theatre Journal* 41, no. 2 (May 1989): 133-54.

24. Ernst Toller. *Man and the Masses*, in Bernard F. Dukore and Daniel C. Gerould, eds., *Avant-Garde Drama: A Casebook* (New York: Thomas Y. Crowell, 1976).

25. Howard Brenton, *Magnificence* (London: Methuen, 1973).

26. Edward Bond, *The Worlds* (London: Methuen, 1976), 76.

27. René Girard, *Violence and the Sacred*. trans. Patrick Gregory (Baltimore and London: Johns Hopkins University Press, 1977), 127-8, 139-42; Julia Kristeva, 'Women's Time', in Nannerl O. Keohane, Michelle Z. Rosaldo and Barbara G. Gelpi, eds., *Feminist Theory: A Critiquue of Ideology* (Brighton: Harvester, 1982), 31-54.

28. Kristeva, 47.

29. Rob Richie, 'Out of the North', Introduction to Ron Hutchison, *Rat in the Skull* (London: Methuen, 19), 5.

30. Eileen Evason. *Hidden Violence* (Belfast: Farset Co-Op Press, 1982). See also Lynda Edgerton, 'Public Protest, Domestic Acquiescence: Women in Northern Ireland', in Rosemary Ridd and Helen Callaway, eds. *Caught up in Conflict: Women's Response to Political Strife* (London: Macmillan in association with the Oxford University Women's Studies Committee, 1986), 61-83; Eileen Fairweather, Roisin Mcdonough, Melanie McFadgean, *Only the Rivers Run Free: Northern Ireland: The Women's War* (London: Pluto Press, 1984); Margaret Fine-Davie, 'A Society in Transition: Structure and Determinants of Attitudes towards Women in Ireland', *Psychology of Women Quarterly* 8, no. 2 (Winter 1983): 113-32.

31. See Laqueur, 214-36.

32. Laqueur, 79-80; Richard Ned Lebow, 'Sectarian Assassination in Northern Ireland', in John Carson, ed., *Terrorism in Theory and Practice* (Toronto: Atlantic Council of Canada, 1978), 48.

33. Christina Reid, *Joyriders and Tea in a China Cup: Two Belfast Plays* (London: Methuen, 1987).

34. Laqueur, 175.

35. Anne Devlin, *Naming the Names*, unpublished transcript of radio version, BBC Written Archives, Caversham, Berks., 83. I am grateful to the BBC for permission to quote briefly from this transcript.

36. In Anne Devlin, *Ourselves Alone* (London: Faber and Faber, 1986), 160, 161, 190-91. Page references to *Ourselves Alone* are also from this volume.

37. W. B. Yeats, 'Remorse for Intemperate Speech' in *The Collected Poems of W. B. Yeats* (London: Macmillan, 1967), 287-8.
38. Heiner Müller, *Hamlet-machine and other Texts for the Stage*, ed. and trans. Carl Weber (New York: Performing Arts Journal, 1984), 50.
39. *Io, Ulrike, Grido* and *Tomorrow's News* are quoted in the translation by Tony Mitchell, *Gambit* 36, no. 9 (1980): 47-53; *La Madre* from *Dario Fo and Franca Rame Workshops at Riverside Studios* (London: Red Notes, 1983), i-xviiii.
40. See Tony Mitchell, *Dario Fo: People's Court Jester* (London: Methuen, 1984); Serena Anderlini, 'Franca Rame: Her Life and Works', *Theater* 17, no. 1 (Winter 1985): 32-9.
41. Anderlini, 33.
42. *Workshops*, 20.
43. Ibid., 7.
44. David Hirst, *Dario Fo and Franca Rame* (London: Macmillan, 1989), 201; see also Sue-Ellen Case, *Feminism and Theatre* (London: Macmillan, 1988) for the view that there is 'no notion of patriarchy as such in Rame's Marxist–feminist texts', 92.
45. Mitchell, 83; Anderlini, 39.
46. Cixous, 'Sorties', in Cixous and Clément, 110.
47. Bonnie Marranca, 'Despoiled Shores: Heiner Müller's Natural History Lessons', *Performing Arts Journal* 32, no. 11 (1988): 22.
48. Ibid., 23.
49. Trevor Griffiths and Jeremy Pikser, *Real Dreams and Revolution in Cleveland* (London: Faber and Faber, 1987). On the Nyack Brinks case see John Castelluci, *The Big Dance: The Untold Story of Kathy Boudin and the Terrorist Family that Committed the Brink's Robbery* (New York: Dodd Mead, 1986); Ellen Frankfurt, *Kathy Boudin and the Dance of Death* (New York: Stein and Day, 1983).
50. *The Judge's Wife* (BBC 1972) deals with state repression of subversive terrorism and *Willie – The Legion Hall Bombings* is based on transcripts of a Diplock Court trial (in which no jury serves) of a boy accused of terrorism in Northern Ireland. See also *Softcops* (1983).
51. Caryl Churchill, 'Interview', *New Theatre Quarterly* IV, no. 13 (February 1988): 10.
52. In Michelene Wandor, ed., *Plays by Women*, Vol. 4 (London: Methuen, 1985).
53. Kristeva, 41-8.
54. Ibid., 47.
55. Ibid., 52.

Index

184